THE EYE IN THE CEILING

THE EYE IN THE CEILING

POEMS BY EUGENE B. REDMOND

HARLEM RIVER PRESS

New York • London

Published for **HARLEM RIVER PRESS** by:
WRITERS AND READERS PUBLISHING, INC.
P.O.BOX 461, Village Station,
New York, New York 10014

Cover Design: Susan Willmarth
Book Design: Windhorse Studio

ISBN 0-86316-308-4 Hardcover
ISBN 0-86316-307-6 Paperback

0 9 8 7 6 5 4 3 2 1

In Memory of my Father's Mother Rosa A. Quinn
&
For the living generations/these Wonderladies
Great Aunt Lily, 90
Daughter Treasure, 20
Grandneice Riana Michelle, 6 months

CONTENTS

THE EYE IN THE CEILING

For *Gerald E. Thomas* and *Donald L. Finkel*

You sit snug in my ceiling
Staring at the room
While insects worship you.

But I can hide you in the night
And your body like a corpse
Loses its heat in seconds.

This time however
Resurrection is simple,
Far simpler than the painful
Mathematics of your birth:

Though in your final death
I'll go through the clumsy
Ritual of unwinding you,

Knowing I could not
Have touched you
In your citadel an hour ago.

SENTRYOFTHEFOUR GOLDENPILLARS

SACRED PLACE

In all sacred places: Brooklyn,
                                  East St. Louis,
                                  Cleveland,
                                  Ibadan,
                                  Watts,
                                  Harlem,
                                  Chicago,
                                  Abijan,
                                  Philly
. . . jazzography is a serious
religion.

Professors,
Teachers,
Audiences
Study invisibly-hooded holymen:
Duke, Bird, Brown, those Milestones who scatted
Drum-ready from African, then New Orleans, loins.

The bandstand/is the altar/
No one blasphemes.
Not even my woman who/
Kneels reverently with me
Each week and/claims
Not to "Understand."

SMOKE AND FIRE

(For *"Smokey"* Bill Robinson)

No standards can gage
This soul-laden airblade;
Poet that makes pain pleasing.

Medicine man from Motown,
Mixing multi-phonic brown,
Rhythmic Sun Ra on the ground —
Tonal bridge to Africa!

Controlled lyric.
Luscious orchestration
Embodied in boyish voice
& beige frame:
Millennia of the strained of the strongest winds
Stripped to a decade of tonal timber.

Baldwin of voice!
The ladies' choice!

Hallelujahs vexed by secular hymns
Hatched and hurled
Through the steeply deep resonance
Of blues sermons.

LOVE NECESSITATES

Grandmother's love
Was sometimes her wrath:
>Quick caresses with switch or ironing cord.

My young unhoned hide knew
Volcanic
Voodoo
Vengeance:
Sting-swift payment for unperformed errands and orders;
Rod and wrath for tarrying too long under Black Bridge.

One did not sass Grandma,
Whose love was *gleam* and *steam*:
Precise preparation (mercy!)
For the Academy of Hard Knocks.

LAST NIGHT

Last night,
The stars scrambled
To one corner of the sky
And chorused
My thoughts
Drenched in rain
Beneath a street lamp.

I was embarassed:
Knowing they knew
Those thoughts
And of you.

But absent of shame,
I was later
Chaka, Zulu-zealous,
Dancing
Through jungle traffic lights,
Spear-teering the night to claim
Your swells and swerves.

Your voice — which came to me
From the darkness —
Died out in even tones
As a pillow met my face
And a knock at the door
Assassinated my dream.

THE *BUM*

Often dogs smell
And track him, as he
Creeps along clean
Alleys,
And hears
Among other things,
The clash of cocktail
Glasses
On patios.

From tin chalices
He
Devises secret
Menus
And borrows
Week-old news.

And sometimes,
The silent eyes
Of patrol cars
Seek out his
Private feast.

In a pillow of heap,
Near the dump,
The moon hides in
The wilderness
Of his dreams.
And a falling star
Is the brightest
Sun he knows.

HEAT WAVE

In summer's morning I stood,
Watching the sun beat flameless
Rhythm down to the swelling
Cadence of the dancing day.

WEDGE WALL, HUGE HAND

(Leffingwell & Franklin Avenues,
St. Louis, Mo.)
For *Luther Mitchell, the Rev. Charles Koen,
Sam Petty* and *Percy Green.*

I

Walls usually obstruct, disrupt
Or hold things up —
Rarely are they pathways to pride and power
Like St. Louis' WALL OF RESPECT,
Black/Built so Blacks can see their (Blackness) tower.

The WALL is a huge hand out-stretched
Or
Turned
On
Its
Edge
Toward the caged overcast;
A hard hand whose horoscopes
Criss-cross
Or
Run parallel in time
3000-years-backwards-in-the-mind;

A hallowed hand
Blood-stained in BLACK BRICK,
Etchings
Of
Unearned
Agony.

II

See: Black people passing by;
Younger girls stop and sigh;
Brick-by brick the faces rise;
Stare, stunned, the stolen eyes.

Ending its day-long glance,
The swollen sun splurges a final stare —
Its stiletto eye having baked bone-hard
The painted faces in the
Skillfully-sculpted hand.

Mounting ladders and platforms
Black artists,
Their solemn sacred tools singing in silence,
Applied pride/pain.

From the valley of asphalt and garbage cans
An uneven line of eyes,
Some leaning against iron knees,
Watched artists moving like
Ancient Egyptian laborers paralyzing sand into
Magnificent faces of Egyptian pyramids.

III

The WALL?
Curiosity turned to reverence!
The ungraspable
Grasped;
Towering untouchability
Over timid stares of the "enemy."

Eye-for-an-eye
For each passerby,
Wooer of wine-washed sidewalks,
The WALL is the people
Is the WALL is
A Whale WALL.

Strikingly still at a vigorous pace;
A haggard beard or a violent face;
Cold, angered stares or a bonnett with lace;
Or Garvey's warm urge: "Up You Mighty Race!"

WALL belongs to the peopleBLACK,
Who come to it,
Like Moslems to Mecca —
Wrested, finally, by truth from colder walls
That dope their minds and give
Them a white Jesus to die for.

The WALL winds miles miles miles miles . . .
And the steel-knuckled fists jut
Like street lamps along the way.

THE ASSASSIN

(Remembering *Malcolm, Martin* and *Fred*)

America's bastard
Child
Peers down the skinnysteel neck
Of a lightning rod whose
Only
Eye
Spits forth fiery acorns of iron
That turn dreams to dung
Hills where
        dictators grow.
devils dabble with death.
          "dreams"
          draw
          destruction.
And the spiritual architects of
Such unsportsmanlike conduct
        sound false alarms
        from an alabaster
           castle
          in D.C.

IN A TIME OF RAIN AND DESIRE

(For any*someplace*one)

a wind-geared cloud of flesh
rained desire into the shiny
rivers of your face:
and turned your arching cheeks into
shores dew-damped and dazzle-dark;
and milk-glazed your twin-mountains
nippled with brown berries;
and liquid-pebbled your tributaries
known as legs;
and overflowed into that pond
(south of your navel and east and west of your thighs)
gripped in grass and precious as the holy (wholee) grail.

and this cloud is lost forever
in the forest of your biology.

PARAPOETICS

(For my former students and writing friends
in East St. Louis, Illinois)

Poetry is an *applied science:*
Re-wrapped corner rap;
    Rootly-eloquented cellular, soulular sermons.

    Grit reincarnations of
    Lady Day
    Bird
    & Otis;
    Silk songs pitched on 'round and rhythmic rumps;
    Carved haloes (for heroes) and asserted maleness:
    Sounds and sights of fire-tongues
    Leaping from lips of flame-stricken buildings in the night.

    Directions: apply poetry as needed.
    Envision.
    Visualize.
    Violate!
    Wring minds.
    Shout!
    Right words.
    Rite!!
    Cohabitate.
    Gestate.
    Inpregnate your vocabulary.
    Dig, a parapoet!

Parenthesis: Replace winter with spring, move Mississippi
   to New York, Oberlin (Ohio) to East St. Louis, Harlem
   to the summer whitehouse. Carve candles and flintstones
   for flashlights.

Carry your poems.
Grit teeth. Bear labor-love pains.
Have twins and triplets.
Furtilize poem-farms with after-birth,
Before birth and dung (rearrange old words);
Study/strike tradition.

Caution to parapoets.
Carry the weight of your own poem.
. . . it's a *heavy lode.*

BARBEQUED CONG: OR WE LAID MY LAI LOW

i

at My Lai we left lint for lawns
feathered with frameless wingless birds,
barbequed and bodyless heads of hair
hanging from the charcoal gazes of burnt huts.

rice-thin hides harbored
flesh-flailing pellets,
unregenerative crops trigger-grown from the trunks of
    branchless
mechanical trees.
as barbeque grills grew hotter, with ghost-hot heat
mothers cooked children and causes
in grease of blood-glazed breasts,
resigned in the weighty whisper that:
"one can only die once."

ii

cannon cut My Lai into fleshy confetti.
pellet-potted half cooked carcasses curing in rice wine.
(rat tat-tat of an idea. souvenirs for patron-saints presiding
    over oil wells.)
flat-faced down in the mud like some unclaimed unnamed
    yet undreamt dream.
while miniature machine-gun minds
mate with mole-holes
on the muddy highways of swamp or swampless night.

iii

"Westward, Whore!"
hear ye . . . hear ye:
a declaration of undeclared causes.
a preamble to constipation and conscription.
dare we overcome?
even arrive?
slightly begin?
go forth against grains before mornings unfold?

iv

my lands! My Lai!
puppet shows and portable pentagods soar or sneak from
      saigon.
Shine came on deck of the mind this morning and said:
"there's a sag in the nation's middle.
which way extends the natal cord —
north or south?"

i lay down my life for My Lai and Harlem.
i lay down my burden in Timbuctu and Baltimore.
we waited long and low
like low-strung studs for My Lai
when we reared and rammed her
with spark-sperm spitting penises
then withdrew westward 6000 miles
(a pacific coffin of the mind between us)
to vex canned good consciences
and claim the 5th Amendment.

DEFINITION OF NATURE

In this stoned and
Steely park,
Love is an asphalt
Fact:
        flowers
        birds
        trees
        rushing or creeping brooks
are framed on walls and tv tubes.

But each night when the city shrinks,
        the stars roof us,
And any bush becomes
        our Bantu wonderland.

THE FALLEN ALTO

In a junk heap
I saw you
Muzzled by a tin can,
Your stained,
Twisted self
No longer
Weaving life from
Course winds
Filtering
Through
A dozen nostrils
And one gaping mouth.

In your
Breathless
But unsunken frame
Insects dwell
And coccoons cling.
You create still!

Would your
Master,
Left voiceless
By your old age,
Know you now?

STRONG LINES

Love lines will last —
From tribal rival
To funnels and tunnels
Of the oldest mind.

Lines etch,
Arrow, narrow through
As lines must.

Lines will last,
Last —
Elastify to include
Martin and Eldridge
In the same stretch.

Lines defy, furrow, infer
More lines in all directions:
Solar biology,
Bodies of water,
Unlocked lands,
Royalty and riffraff,
Ebony and mulatto,
Palm-readings,
Longitude and latitude,
Spinal columns and raised buttocks.

Lines will last,
Encage,
Care for,
Until the day of battle.

CONSIDER LONELINESS
AS THESE THINGS

CONSIDER LONELINESS AS THESE THINGS

Consider loneliness a lull,
As some secret space that jails the mind,
As a circumstantial melody: the blues of
Wretchedness or the blues of joy;
As some totem of penitence or pity or pride,
Sagging from the neck like a lead medallion
Or a dead bird:
Spinning out,
Spinning out wire-threads or hardfeathers of confinement;
As a hypnotist, eye-blind, with psychic sight
And strength to unleash the lances of unexpurgated pain,
Of unquelled thought-quakes, or Watusi-tall dreams.
Consider loneliness as these things.

Consider loneliness as a weaver of want,
As a giver of needs undefined,
As some ancestral repository
For a personal mythic tablet;
As a nerve, nudged overgently —
Or laced with worry;
As a womb, wailing out its
Liquid waifs, its tight lips waiting,
Waiting . . .
As a tyrant, timeless and elastic —
Consider loneliness.

LOOKING THROUGH LIQUID

Joy.
Envious wind gathering
     at your Himalayan thighs.

Joy.
Winding molding, cone-shaping
     vieing for v-shaped prize.

Joy.
Serene self-of-yourself bonelessly
     limp at chilled sunrise.

Joy.

SUNDOWNING

Clouds fall like splashed ink
Against the sky.

Which is moving:
The car or the world?

The day cools.
Evening refrigerates our thoughts.
Our brains stop boiling.

You descend upon me with the night chill,
Peripatetic and omni-dark.

I drive one-handed.
You match point with number on radio,
Mumble celestial jargon in my ear,
And flip my fly zip
Back and forth.

Radio,
Road hum,
Leering lights careen on
Fender and forehead.
Face and Foreskin.
Your eyes spheres of fire!
Do you work some
African magic on me?

SECOND COMING

Fire! Fire!
Where, oh where, will you be
When flames go on that global spree?

When Earth's crotch and crop catch fire
And the planets won't piss on the pyre?
But wait for echoes from the ashen urn:
"Oh didn't it, didn't it burn!
Oh, my Lord, didn't it burn!"

When a sleazy planet shaken from nap
         Asks,
"Burn? Burn? Oh dear, has earth got the clap?"

CARRYOVER

(Thinking about *Jimmy Dixon, Clarence Nelson* and
Darnell Sullivan)

I have been tattooed for life:

A thought called EAST ST. LOUIS

Is etched on each Island of my Brain.

EAST ST. LOUIS will rise!

Will rise from the muddy gutty Mississippi.

Will rise disguised as AFRICA.

WILL RISE!

WILL RISE THROUGH THE MIND-EYES OF

hustler & hairdresser
teacher & astronaut

athlete and anchorman
mathematician and mime

waiter & dishwasher
elk & mason

cabdriver and architect
hodcarrier and cartoonist

maid & mechanic
doctor & undertaker

journalist and judge
bluesician and be-bopper

preacher & plumber
gardener & garbage collector

violinist and veterinarian
griot and gutbucketeer

EAST SAINT ain't dead yet!

I've got the scars and tattoos to prove it!

Can't you feel the yeast in the air!

THE ATMOSPHERE IS STARVING

Moon tune.
Spatial rhythm.
Gorgeous galaxy.
Otherwhereness.
(I pity emptiness of
space or stomach.)

Song of the ether:
Feathery phonics for speeding phallic
Splitting molecular madness.
The universe has no more cherry
And Harlem no more food.

Moon tune.
Coal-dust colored faces
Copper coat the night.
"Might is right!"

Spaceship: gouge through malnutrient
Stomachs; let no lord of testament
Cause you lag.
(What is the formula for manufacturing man?)

Moon: don't waste the milk of the cow that mounts you.
Moon tune: 24 billion leagues above the sea
(and still unanchored and unsung).

Forgive this rude intestinal growl
Interrupting your congressional symphony.

LITTLE PEOPLE

In the omen-cloaked chill
Of the October wind,
Brittle little legs snap, crackle and bend
But never crumble.
Books, grapsed in belts and boxes,
Are pulled reluctantly along
Like low-land cows after grazing.

Cool Black cavaliers, their struts
Developed to 9-year perfection, glory be!,
Apply the precision of Bo-Jangles
To jubilant jaunts.

Moon children confronting late dawn:
Night people streaming to meet the sun;
Sunrise on sunset's hindparts,
Carcass of the moon, the day carts.

Little people don't contrive,
Contribute to,
War — they just inherit it.

THE FIRE INSIDE

Whether the weather is windy or rainy,
Stormy or sane with average sun,
I express some eastern elation at creation;
I express distress (sometimes) at my inability
To dispel the mental pell-mell of
        Heaven or Hell
Or the knife of life.

These things, however, cause me no prolonged
Strife, especially since I know they
Do not phase the African.
Besides, I tell myself, my understanding
Ancestors will forgive me
For such sacrilegious thought:
Bought albeit with western currency.

Each day, I trace strand: lines along hand and land.
Whence came I?

A change in weather is rather well accepted
After wind has awakened and unwound my ethnic
Consciousness and I am too much with Africa.
Lord! lord!

RIVER OF BONES
AND FLESH
AND BLOOD

RIVER OF BONES AND FLESH AND BLOOD

(MISSISSIPPI)

For *Doris Cason*

River of time:
Vibrant vein,
Bent, crooked,
Older than the Red Men
Who named you;
Ancient as the winds
That break on your
Serene and shining face;
One time western boundary of America
From whose center
Your broad shoulders now reach
To touch sisters
On the flanks

River of truth: Mornings
You leap, yawn 2000 miles,
And shed a giant joyous tear
Over sprouting, straggling
Hives of humanity;
Nights you weep
As the moon, tiptoeing
Across your silent silky
Face, hears you praying
Over the broken backs
Of black slaves who rode,
Crouched and huddled,
At your heart in the bellies
Of steamships.

River of Memory:
Laboratory for Civil War
Boat builders
Who left huge eyes of steel
Staring from your sullen depths;
Reluctant partner to crimes
Of Ku Klux Klansmen;
River moved to waves
Of ecstasy
By the venerable trumpet
Of Louis Armstrong.

River of Bones:
River of bones and flesh —
Bones and flesh and blood;
The nation's largest
Intestine
And longest conveyor belt;

River MISSISSIPPI:
River of little rivers;
River of rises,
Sometimes subdued
By a roof of ice, descending finally
On your Southward course
To spit
Into the Gulf
And join the wrath
Of larger bodies.

EPIGRAMS FOR MY FATHER

(John Henry Redmond, Sr.)

I

Fatherlore: papa-rites, daddyhood;
   Run & trapsong: Search & dodgesong.
Steelhammeringman.
Gunbouter; whiskeywarrior.
Nightgod!
Moonballer/brawler grown old.
Slaughterhouse/river mackman:
Hightale teller & totempoleman.

II

Wanderer across waters:
Folkbrilliance & Geniusgrit;
Railraging railsplitter:
Railrage! Railrage!
IC & BM&O & MoPac & Midnight Special:
Freight train . . . . . . bring my daddy back!

III

Stone-story. The story of stone, brokenbricks —
Rocks hurled in pleasure & rage,
Pebbles soft & silent:
Home-dome is a blues-hard head.

IV

45-degree hat, Bulldurham butt bailing from lips;
Gabardine shining shining shining
Above white silk socks —
      satin man

satin man
silksure & steelstrong
hammerhold on life
hammerhold on life

V

Sun-son. Stonebone. Blackblitz.
Fatherlore. Struggledeep: Afridark, Afrolark,
   daddydepth —
   Riverbottom song.

GODS IN VIETNAM

Mechanical oracles
Dot the sky,
Casting shadows on the sun.
Instead of manna
Leaflets fall
To resurrect coals, dead
From the week's bombing.

Below in the
Jungle,
Flaming altars buckle under
Prophecies;
And smoke whimpers
In the west wind.

Dry seas hide the
Cringing fold
While fishermen Leap from clouds,
Nets blooming on their
Lean bodies.

The sun slumps,
Full;
Before it sleeps,
Solemn chaplains come,
Their voices choked
In suspicious silence.

SEPTEMBER IN MARCH

No sun, no clouds,
And the day is
Suddenly clear.

Flat winds move like
Wide unseen walls
Against the buildings
And the people.

Skirts flutter in
Embarassment, while
High-crown and porcupine
Hats and wing-like caps
Tumble in the streets.

On the main drag —
Extending out over numerous
Shops and stores —
Large canvas canopies
Waver and subside.

Small whirlpools can be
Seen where-ever dust and
Other particles collect.

I cannot see the wind.

CITY NIGHT STORM

For *L. Wendell Rivers*

Dark winds kiss the walls
And split on the blades of corners;
The burning eyes of the city dance
In a thousand rusting skulls.

Twisting trees listen to
The pulses of tired streets;
And birds miss their landings.

A fleeing garbage can suddenly
Scares a sleeping cat; and a drunk,
Held upright by the headwind,
Slouches into daylight.

The condescending moon says nothing,
But coasts half-seen along night's ceiling;
And the angry, chilling breath rushes over
Darkness, like waters over a fall.

THE 18 HANDS OF JEROME HARRIS

Drumsticks masturbate in his hands!
As over-sexed audiences follow suit,
Their hot flesh flinching, meanwhile, under
The patter of penis-shaped wooden feet.

18 hands sound songs of stones with dried bones!
Polished branches, baked in African blood,
Tap tunes for Hard times:
Hard times for babies leaping
From the beat of black bellies —
The howl of an ancient echo —
Hung in the brick-steel-glass-weedy
Throat of urban and rural jungles.

The branches have many personalities:
Heels hounding hostile pavements in search of jobs,
Fans,
Drills,
Hammers that haunt ear drums,
Whips and arrows aimed at
Sailing cymbals,
Igniting them with
Flashes from flaming eyes.

18 hands in fierce flight or pained pursuit:
Heating and bothering the delirious drums
Like a teenager who traps his ripe prey
In some dark hallway.

The branches cling fast or climb slowly
Like heavy hands of tower clocks
Announcing the day's age.

They move in Harris' hands,
Timed and intent,
Through
Prayers!
Battles!
Great bodies of blood
Driven as by daredevils
And horse-herders constantly at some finish line.

Or they tread cautiously
As hands curing animal carcasses
Dying for drums in the sun.

18 hands, holding blood-blessed branches,
Make hollow drums deep and long
Like the unwritten diaries of Katherine Dunham
Whose sacred legs still straddle continents.

The solo ends in drums of living flesh;
Applause shatters straying silence;
Later, as ladies get up to go pee
And smoldering eyes rise up to see,
The thin skin of the drums lies quivering
Like a young woman just well sanctified,
Beneath the fallen eyes and unarched shoulders
Of Jerome Harris:
Prophet of skin and tin!
Teller of tales!
Keeper of time!
Holder of blood-blessed branches!

Drummer with 18 hands!

SPRING IN THE JUNGLE

You tiptoed
Naked
Into the
Jungle
Of my soul;

And the underbrush
Divided before
You.

A choir of birds
Grew
Understandably
Silent;

And I stood
Beside
Myself with joy
And watched
The season grow
To
Spring

Let my soul
Be always
Green
And sprinkled with
Daisies;

Let there be
Dew for the sun to bathe in
And winds to do rituals
For the
Moon.

TWILIGHT

Her *mojo* dimmed to a mutter
Her *firehead* shaved of its flames
Her *bloodpace* slowed to a crawl
Her *magic* brimming with names
Her *queenquilts* trimmed to a shawl
Her *lightning* chilled to a flicker
Her *power* calmed to a call

INVASION OF THE NOSE

For *Joseph Harrison*

His nose was his radar,
His eyes icy darts that moved faster than speed-of-sound
      jets.
He could rap like a pneumatic drill!
Or croon like Smokey Bill when the occasion arose.

He was a cool,
Hip,
OFF-INTO-A-THING dude,
Mellow —
In yellow silk undershirts
Exposed through unbuttoned
Jerseys from Greenfields.

"Dig this, man," he would say,
"I ain't tripping with no jive-ass-bitch."

He stood/hung/laid/dealt
On the corner,
Bent in a 20-degree angle,
One hand clutching the wrist
Of the opposite arm behind his back.
And he could dart-like-lightning
Into a 5 ft. female's ear.

His popping-tongue titillated the titties
Of other men's wives
And awed adolescent girls;
Middleaged ladies gave him
Fat-fees for his flailing fingers.

He was an acknowledged action eater
Who was hip to *Trane,*
Bird,
Prez,
Jug Head,
Duke,
Count,
Ray Charles, James Brown and *Howlin' Wolf.*

But one day
She found a hole in his soul,
Put a furtile fang in his thang

And his nose grew like blunderbuss barrels.

BLACKFEST

For *Jim & Lindell Penn*

African nightfires dance and cackle;
      And our neon bodies are Christmas Trees
Brushing against the walls of the dark:
      Now, children of the *whirl*,
Come! Congregate, shed sweat with us,
      And *swirl!*

BLACK COMMUNITY: MIND & MIRROR

I

MIND

"Got a boogaloo in your brain!"
— K. Curtis Lyle

Take *long* breaths & strides,
Stroke & straddle an ocean:
         Sitting — thinking — running
Thru the book of *yourself,*
The book of the dead
The living & the *yestermorrow.*

To the sky's skull
To the earth's belly-center
To the eyeballs of oceans
To the tonsils of birds & storms
To the navel of the sun
Stroke-stroke-stroke-stroke
Full strength to what Stevie Wonder called
"Yester-you" & *"Yester-me";*

To *self,* sunk deep in blues and praise songs of the mind,
Cuddled in the applauding waves of that *last river,*
Brooding in a battlefield named memory,
Thumping in a motherdrum called Africa,
Styling in a footstop, banjoboogie, tambourine,
         boogaloo & *mood indigo,*
Swelling in a socket or pocket or rocket of earth
Where unbranded brains think sea-size thoughts:
         In a book of song!
         In a book of dance!
         In a book of style!

In an air-sea where stars caucus
In a mind-act
In a mobile-thought
In the armour & shield of ancestral corridors
In the hooves of ideas prancing & dancing in the mirror of
    the multitude!
Take *long* breaths & strides,
Stroke & straddle an ocean:
    An ocean of song!
    An ocean of dance!
    An ocean of style!
Sitting — thinking — running
Thru the book of *yourself*,
Thru the book of the dead, the living
& the *yestermorrow.*

II
MIRROR

Mirages of the mind rend,
    Sometimes send mad,
The mirrors of the soul:
But way shape form & fashion
    Come, *spirit-driven,*
From glossy black forests:
"This little light of mine . . . I'm gonna let it *shine!*"
    Let it *shine!*
    Let it *shine!*
    Let it *shine!*
Lance-like *yestermirrors* of toil, tall tales & talismen,
Of mojo-men and sledgehammering horrors,

Of glassy grease & the sweat of unswum rivers to cross.
Of spear-dash glint & the razor-rove of eyes;
From the massforehead comes:
   Lucid light!
   Oh luminescence of the soul!
Yestermirrors illuminate the soul of song,
Illuminate the *self,* sunk deep in *Black Gloss,*
Deep in licorice lacquer, deep in the throb-photo of
   daddydrum;
Night arches into Africa:
   Sounds are drawn . . . oh ebony mirror!
   Sounds are drawn . . . oh beams to bear!
   Sounds are drawn . . . oh night shellacked!
This *mirror,* this *mantel:* light-lances bouncing from
   foreheads & halls,
Rebounding, resounding in the bellybutton of the drum:
Clatter of ghetto teeth, clicks of tongues,
Ancestral echoes, songs of dust & hurt, bluesful rime:
   acoustical *mirrors!*

Yestermirrors are *yester-us* are *yestermorrows.*
   Let them shine!
   Let them shine!
   Let them shine!

THE BASTARD

these shores, these agonies

Across the white desert
Sludges the
Bastard,
His Black face upstaging
Night
As he weeps into the
Cold
Ears of a father.

On his brow
Lie stillborn the hopes
Of 3 centuries
And on the face of his
Brothers
The rebuttal.

Beside the oasis,
Mother offers a
Sword
To his burning
Tongue
While orphans cast
Lot for his inheritance.

POETIC REFLECTIONS ENROUTE TO, AND DURING, THE FUNERAL AND BURIAL OF HENRY DUMAS, POET

I
FLIGHT TO NEW YORK

> *"I am ready to die"*
> — Henry Dumas in
> *"Our King Is Dead,"* 1968.

A passive sea of white foam
Separates this swift and fleshless bird
From the black earth that waits for *Henry Dumas, poet.*
At 30,000 feet up
The mind has plenty of space to wander:

Just think!
A second-story world —
No steps, no ladders.
Meanwhile onto aluminum-covered wings the sun leaps
And breaks into a thousand heated needles
As my head averts,
With a twist,
Its stabbing, staring presence.

Now we soar through angry winds,
Bouncing unpredictably like a football
Turned loose in some smooth, open place.
But the pilot guides the bird cautiously
Through the ordeal while our hearts,
At first hung like anxious medallions around our necks,
Resume their natural places;

And the cries, before dignifiedly choked,
Die forever in our throats.

We the living:
Are we some majestic, royal party?
A high tribunal judging the lower world?
Gods? Goddesses?
Who is above and who is below?
. . . the pilot's voice and then
A view of Staten Island.
We nose through the second sea to caress LaGuardia Field.
The stewardess smiles at the passenger sitting
Alone in the rear: "Pretty good landing in the rain,
        wasn't it?"
She's a company girl, the poet muses — a robot with nice
        legs.
Parts and rhythms of the painful puzzle fall together on the
        ground.
But I must hurry to the funeral in the Bronx.
Amid sounds and sights, I near the cab and am terrified
        at my image
In the glossy surface of its wet body.

And on the way to McCall Funeral Home
I try in vain to figure out who I am.

II
THE FUNERAL

> *"A Black Poet is a preacher."*
> — *Statement by Henry Dumas, 1968.*

The balding black preacher
Read and ad-libbed

Before a lamp that threw
A cone-shaped light up into his face.
The eulogy was brief,
The man was eloquent and magnificent
In dark robes: *a poet saluting a poet.*
Occasionally his eyes fell
Like heavy weights
On the casket to his right,
Draped in a United States flag.
Dumas had served in the Air Force.
The articulate preacher had not known the poet
But the poet's mother.
One could see that the circumstances of the killing
Had undermined his faith.

He sought a way out: Equating the poet with "Mr.
Lincoln."
He also knew the poet wrote:
"This young man will survive
In his stories and poems," the bowed audience was
Reminded.
"He walked upright like a man . . .
There are mysteries; life is a mystery,
Death is a mystery."
The radiant black man of cloth
Was unpretentious; he broke with tradition — promising
No alternatives to death.
Seemingly unaware of heaven or hell, he suggested simply
    "a last resting place."
Those in the chapel stared intently, bleakly
Into their own thoughts.
Outside the skies cried for the dead black bard.

III
FORTY-FIVE MINUTES TO THE CEMETERY

Rain,
Earlier in East St. Louis and now in New York.
The skies continue to mourn for the fallen poet and warrior,
Mojo-handler and prophet.

Four passengers in the fourth car,
Divided by a generation of intellect,
But feeling a common pain,
A mutual bewilderment:
Four grit faces of the oppressed.

The dead poet rode in the first car
But was present in the whole train:
Smiling in approval at our candid talk.
Dumas was like that. "Man, let's just tell it ," he used to say.
Yes, and he had given direction to the
Pen of the younger poet earler that morning
Several stories up, adrift in a big bird of steel.

Our talk was shop:
"Henry and I finished Commerce High School together,"
The driver intimated.
A middleage friend of the poet's mother said:
"They're killing off all our good men; I tell ya, a black man
Today speaks his piece at the risk of losing his life."

New Yorkers talk differently than East St. Louisans,
The younger poet observed to himself.

The cars of the procession,
Standing out with bright eyes against the dim day,
Sped cautiously toward Farmingdale National Cemetery
Where white marble headstones stood mute and macabre:
Quite geometrically arranged in a sprawling well kept
ocean of green.

Again talk: "They're slaughtering our boys in Vietnam,"
the middleage lady
Quipped; "this graveyard will be filled up soon."
A bus carrying the Army Honor Guard joined us at the
entrance to the cemetery.

The guard gave a trifling, sloppy salute to the fallen poet
Who had served his country.
More talk as we departed the graveside:
"Young David walks just like his daddy,"
The driver informed us about Dumas' eldest son.

"Neither of the boys understand what's going on,"
The driver's mother noted.
"Who does?" the young poet asked himself.

A confession from the middleage lady: "Can't cry no more.
Just won't no more tears come out — all dried up."
Her eyes looked like worn rubies, inquisitive jewels
Polished to worn perfection
By having seen many things
Including the dead poet's "good looking"
Remains.
The driver echoed her: "Henry was beautiful; he looked
Just like he was sleep."

The driver was a spirit lifter, also an interior observer:
"Henry thought too deep for the average person."

Upon leaving the cemetery
The procession broke up.
Cars bearing license plates from various places sped on or
    turned off,
Went their way and my way.

The skies lifted their hung heads.
Mrs. Dumas smiled finally and played with her sons,
David and Michael.
The boys, cast in the same physical mold as their father,
Were impeccably dressed.

GEARS OF THE GLOBE

For *Gabriel Bannerman-Richter*

African moon cartwheels in the night's eye;
African moon stalls in the clouds;
Black sod nods
As earth's rods,
Gears and chains
Are oiled by dewspray
And rootjuice,
Voodoo'd for another day.

DISTANCE

I am still on fire.

The flames in my veins and heart
Boil blood and burn hissing-hot.

Yet my time is inched on
By the realization of each new
Gleam-in-a-father's-eye.

My wrinkled oval sacks
Have pumped up a sea of come
Up through a mercenary-muscle
Into vaginas, wet towels and mouths.
But each sapping of the glistening love-sauce
Creates a new supply
Like the Phoenix Bird that rises from its own ashes.

More and more, like James Brown,
I find myself saying "I used to . . . . there was a time."

The mind grows younger and remembers:
The poetic but unprophetic words of my grandmother
    as she played
Tick-tack-toe on my butt with an ironing cord:
"You little black bastard; Nigger, you won't live to be 21
With your mannish tail";
Parking piously in the park to finger-fuck and poke pussy
    after dark;
Coming three times-in-a-row;
Crawling through wives' windows;

Palating pills, inhaling hashish, sucking syrup,
And gurgling O'Grady in a 1-2-3-4 fashion.

The items mount memory's totem pole:
The wild gossip of *Lady Day;*
The trips of *Yard Bird;*
The passion and elegance of *Mr. B;*
The legacy of *Chano Pozo;*
The hum of *Midnighters,*
Drifters,
Coasters
And *Orioles;*
The mood, mind and myths of *Miles.*

A single life,
A daily diet of death and
Under the bludgeoning of the slave drivers call
I am bound and thrown
At the feet of a white Christ
Where vultures stab and snap with putrid beaks at my
eye balls.

I now know distance and dread:
rivers and voices
freedom in a cage
freedom in a cage

Distance calls. In my secret soul heroes have always been
Black.
But America raised me on
John Wayne

Shirley Temple
And Tarzan.

America gave me distance!
America gave me distance!

Now, while I am still on fire,
I ache in anger to get home.

WALKING ONE DAY IN BATON ROUGE, LOUISIANA
(Saturday, July 3, 1971)

Walking one day in Baton Rouge,
Fresh shrimp frying in my head,
The wind, suddenly, gored me
In my tracks and pressed me
Against a wall of stiff air —
And, then, she was there!
Her presence an oakhold,
An ache, a gnaw, an admonishment:
Sweet teethbared arrogant
Spirit held out like a lance of hardest steel
Or a shield of wry smiles;
This presence an impaled beauty,
An impartial stare:
    And me — *with my need of nail* —
    Wanting to hit so hard it hurt.
Here in this flamespace,
This selfdisintegrating daydream,
My teeth and tongue boiling in butterflavored spit,
Windwalls so thick so thrustful:
    And me — *with my need of nail* —
    Wanting to hit so hard it hurt.
And the wind, treasonous and triumphant,
It pressed me to my tracks — like a quicksand
Of slowsuction:
    And me — *wanting to hit so hard it hurt.*

GRANDMOTHER

(Winter,1966)
Remembering *Rosa A. Quinn*

She is a child
Whose dark eyes no longer
Divine the hidden fever
Or fathom rough lies
On a little black face.

Sullen walls
Are now haunted by stained
Portraits of Christ,
The dusty monuments
To her silent desertion.

A pair of callous knees
Record four-score years
Of daily soliloquies.
Chanted into
An arch of scaly hands.

And she unstops no more
The choked sewer
In the sunken street;
Nor sandbags in the rain
Mud threatening the *four o'clocks*.

Muscles that used to saw
And fashion logs into quilt-trees
Now sag

Like her long since
Shrunken breasts.

She is a strange child at 86;
Who relishes the taste of peppermint
And the somber hum of spirituals

THREE FROM THE OBSERVATORY

I

The gagged sun groped half-strength
through prisonous clouds:
flitting foams holding it
in psychedelic confinement.

II

The day was receding
down the slope of its
own beginning; slowly
winding withinward along the tapered tail
of its time-funnel
towards beingless;
beginning to cool to shrink
to grow grayly and blackly
into the mouth of
its licorice-colored birth.

III

As the moon nibbled
at the day's carcass,
and the stars leaped to perch
on night's lamp posts,
I, rebel enshrouded,
pissed in the street.

SONGS FROM AN AFRO/PHONE

"... take the sculptor who carves a mask ... while this sculptor carves, he sings a song, he sings a poem and he weaves a poem. And there you see the significant and the significance. The image and the idea in symbiosis ... the tradition of the word-word. ... priests and artists must have the gift of imagery, of symbolism, of rhythm."

— Léopold Sédar Senghor
President of Senegal, Poet and
Philosopher of Negritude

TO SOME GONE FIGHTERS I HAVE KNOWN:
>Herbert A. Jackson, Henry Dumas, Taylor Jones III,
W. Nicholas Bowie, Lyon Herbert;

TO SOME EARLY IDOLS I WATCHED TO SEE HOW TO
'KEEP ON GETTIN' UP' — EVEN FROM MY OWN
SPILT BLOOD:
>Golden "Perk" Perkins, Levi May,
Jesse "Tucks" Edwards, McKinleuy "Ham" Logan,
Mel "Big Track" Ship, Willie Fair,
Roger "Frag" Hudson, Jr., Harold "Prince" House,
Carey "Watashi" Washington, William "Jug" Leggs,
Ted "Pop" Miles;

TO SOME FIGHTERS/TEACHERS I KNOW STILL:
>Charles Koen, Alvin Batiste, Fred Teer,
Homer Randolph, Wyvetter Younge, Al Geiger,
Joseph Harrison, Robert "Bob" Hoover,
Katherine Dunham.

BROTHERSONG: COMPOSITION FOR MY MIRROR

For *John Henry Redmond, Jr.*

1

Dear mirror:
Dearer mirror . . . shatterless glass;
Shining and shouting back my me/my me;
Autobiography caught in nostalgic corners of mind light;
In the needlelight of the son; in the lasergrace
Of the sun: kinetic kin-note,
Life-lunging lyric,
Ringdancer and Hatmaker;
Mani/gear knuckled, buckled,
Fastened, seatbelted
Onto a boldshouldered manblade.

2

Dear mirror:
Coming, humming clearer to me;
Whose brown body is a song
Whose brown body is a slug
Halfhumming halfwhistling "One Mint Julep":
"One early moanin'
While I was wawking . . ."
Mansong on a morning of shutters and chillbumps;
Bluesbalm percolating a morning of potbellies:
"Coal-l-l Man! Coal-l-l-l!
Coal-l-l Man! Coal-l-l-l!"

3

Dear mirror:
BeBopping "Bird" digger;
Grinding against Miles Music
As waiter, as mackman, as rentmaker,
As bikebaron and brownbattler;
As moorish sailor returning to Spain
In Afro-American frame;
As maker of songboy and songgirl.

4

Dear mirror:
Shining back might and moan
Shining back man and moon
Beating back song and saga
Ballrooming back blues and booze
Shiningback! Shiningback! Shiningblack!
Gibraltric shoulder in a sandseepage;
Light-anchor in a nightmare's mouth;
Plougher/planter of seeds in the stomach of tomorrow.

AXE SONG; SWORDPHONE

For *Julius Hemphill*

HEAR:
Razorblades break and brocade air,
Hew wood and hack wind;
Hear sculptures of your mind . . .
Here strictures of your mind
Squeal or mutter some knife of speech of sound:
Give poise and drumcall to the air,
Bequeath breath a bolt of song: *riffin' riffin'*,
Grind anger into genius,
Glean from wrath an order, a throne: *riffin' riffin'*,
Sew threads of sounds
Through ancestral garments —
Needle, knife or handclap split
Natal cords and you blow babies into life:
Cutting to heal
Bleeding to seal: *riffin' riffin'*
       Blooding a muscle of notes,
       Hurling air-axes through stormwaters,
       Fishing for fireblades in an ocean of air.

SÉNOR PEPÉ'S PROMENADE

For *Joe Gauthier*

Food frets/promenades at *Sénor Pepé's*
    Refried beans/
A goldenhostess in breastsmiles
Wearing restraining wall of knit
       /sweatered senorita/
Swelling up/out horizontal mountains
       /miniatured/
Burritos/
Enchiladas tucked in tortillas/
Mexicali beer
       /the sun liquefied & bottled/
          and *sheGlows*
SheGlows, strung like flamenco melody
Rolling over the shores
       /slamming the beaches/
Of my ears;
From sunfractured frames/walls/
Mute as history and motionless as murals,
       /girldancers; sombrero'd senors stare/
Guarding this tradition
       /this hummingheat toil/
This KnifeForkPlate chatter and clatter,
       this feast and fiesta:
ChaCha-spiced lips
Smacking, wacking away at Mexican scrumptiousness;
"Wa-atch eet seen-yore, thee plate eeze hot"
The waiter wises
       /from a blue vestjacket snaps/
Lowers baked dish to tablecloth

                /blue/
Straddling carpet
                /blue/
Whose designs/topo-rhymes scurry/wigglehurry like tributaries
                /blue/   sky
And the room hatdances/
Drowning in Flamenco guitar
Glowing in Flamenco melody
Buttered in beangrease
                /and *sheGlows in* Mexicali Beer/

SONGS FROM AN AFRO/PHONE

For *Darryl Redmond*

Afro/phone
      voice-in-a-veil/trumpet Gabriel-ing slavery's burial
Threading the needle's slit/
Taming the weather's spit;
Tiptoeing on a straightpin's roof
Through a soprano storm!
      /on an alto windblade/

Cymbals of lightning climbing clouds!
A bassly thunder strung in the land's groin!
The eye of the storm is a narrowhum/noddinghum,
The wipe of the wind a colossal laugh/flammable cough/;
As the footfalls of trillionth-trillionth man
Flail the drumbelly of the globe/
Flirt with a hum that is seasonal solemnity.

Afro/phone . . . tree-trumpet fluting galaxial voices;
Cosmo horn and urn calling:
      Leaf-reed and lyrical!
      Reed-leaf and miracle!
Fantasy and finale of man forced/
Danced through wooden lips,
Through gravel jaws/
Across rivertongues/
Up from lakelarynx/
With mountainMagic churning stone to stereo coolness
In the hollow between these global titties
      between these global ditties:

That from the Afro/phone stream
That from the Afro/phone scream
That from the Afro/phone strike
Strum fire
            /blasting the furnace of the sun/

SWIFTSONG

For *Isaac Hayes*

A BluesBlindingSpeed!
          /BreakNeckBlackness!/
An ice-man
          /sun-sure/
Moaning;
A grouphood *gone-ing, lone-ing,* yeahhh!
A swordsong; a reedvoice;
Swift, *Jim!*, swift and stiff:
Stiffer than stone, *blood*, and colder — *chilly-er!*
Gittin' up soulo . . .
Gettin' down so-high . . .
My My My, Sister swiftJones, My My:
Pass the salad and the sisters, please!
Pass the pride/the buttered girl/gold!
Slap my hands into flapjack soul!
          hand/
                    me/
                    down/
                              them/
                                        blues
Rituals revolving at the speed of sound!
Swiftsong is a bloodclock called blues:
BreakNeckBlackness jammin' joy
          /jitterbugging the sun/
Gittin' up *soulo, Jim!*, being reel swift/
Stiff, slick with the grease/speed of the blues:
Jetdance, swift!
          IKE-kon/
                    Swift!

BLUES-TONE #1

For *Sherman Fowler*

From the ashnight of a *bluesfire*
I emerge a tune of history
A moon melody
A mood bar, a diminuendo spirit
Smoke-laureling and snorting *yestertorches* of wisdom/
Fireblades of wisdom on some beach
Bleached *Nth*-white:
   "Flame-seed, Somewhere, Somehow!"
As a tooltune of history
Cultivating/hoeing and harvesting
Little flames for larger fires
That I will bank to burnsongs
That I will sing to urn-sized loves:
   "O fire-song, O seed, O need!"
As a field of flame-seeds
Where ashes of a love-urn grow;
Flakes of passion under *bluefires*
Under *bluesfires* lipping the coat-tail,
The frayedhem of tomorrow: the *bluesglow*
The *blueglow*, the *blackglare* of desire,
Of wish and of wail:
   "Fire-song, Bluestongs, Someday soon!"

BLUES-TONE #2

For *Jerry Herman* and *Other Black Writers*

Blues-tone/blues-drone on a typewriter:
    "Blue Rites! Blue Rites!"
Blue thumps of drumpen pleading/
Exhorting paper screens —
Rap-tap! drums of inundation, of syncopation
And a bodybeat/ an ideo-beep in ideophone/
A drivinghome, a drive-suite
Against the eternal mattress/the clay carpet
Of eternal rhythm/of divine rhyme
Flowing from feet/street
Into sacred fingers/
Fingers spilling folkhymns across a giant ellipsis
And crocheting riddles through crossworded weapons:
    "Blue Rites! Blue Rites!"
Fingers bledblue through penprayer
Through type-key cadence: churchchant and dogboogie —
Rap-tap! and centuries collide or speed by
Rap-tap! and ancestors swarm or sugar-thought the head
Rap-tap! and the type is a tear, making words sag
Rap-tap! and urge is an owl, staring from weewee words in the
    night;
Blue-tone on a typewriter: *Rap-tap!*
Breastplated, soul-insulated and bledblue;
Heartflamed fingers scratching, *RAP-TAP!*,
Scraping the epidermis of the mind.

BIG SISTER SONG

For *Ethel Mae Redmond*

Helping us grow up-out-in guillotined/stillbore
Those jewel-laden years in the mind of darkdiamonds
That was/is you, solid-set and lightning-lit.

We, the younger-elders, knew-and-knew-not the source
/even as we sought the sauce/
Of your corrugated concern, your candid care,
And of your vigils and visits by-bus, by-foot-, by-laugh, by-tear.

And "Mae" came constantly, a sober sun, carting smiles
Fixed as forms/flexible as flames licked by cynical winds;
In cotton dresses, "May", carrying bags — bearing guessed-at-
June joys;
Came clocklike with questions, with cautions:
Measles? Mumps? Books? Shoes? Kindling? Coal for the stove?

Littled lives, hop-scotching/patty-caking on love,
Sprouted/flung toward this grand sistermother, toward Black
Upstance; across lore, across land, across life —
To laugh and to lash — *to a song of branching, a song of sooning.*

LONE SONG

First fears, first tears on autumn window pains,
Left over hurt from summer
/dregs of Illinois madness/

California song is subtle sting;
California chill is quiet, coy — cat/walk —
Not noisy and nervous like midwestern winters.

My mood, then, often comes — is drumhummed — by mail;
My fury, my flame, my fidget caught postcard-quick,
Caught and cornered,
/bulletinboarded/shored upon saltfilled tomorrows/

Brother Sister Nephew Niece:
Vital vibes on wire, on lyre — kincords/
Bloodcords of sounds or strings: spontaneous
COMBUSTION of blood inside *trees*, inside *seeds* and *shells* —
Inside xylophones, telephones and saxophones.

LOVE SONG

In the madness, in the *madsting*
Of windherds grabbing
              /goring mud & dust/
At you gallops
              /in gulps/
Or flameforests gathering you together
In coppergreen bundles of fire-grass
Or jetbreath collecting you in the arms
Of its lumberous storms,
In the *madsting* of hell-beheld,
I maintain my cool:
              Knowing that my promise, baby,
Is a mountain/is a sun of consistency
Is a doorknob of nature
Is a rainstorm of romance —
Here, then, this song:
Know my love, kinetic and corrugated;
Know this ocean of need, this fever of urgency;
Know this center that is quietchant,
Clumsy-Core,
Yet roar/distant and immediate/of *secret choruses*
              /*"Madsting! Madsting!"*/
Of vital forces.

ITCH-SONG

(The Black lawyer seen as warrior at the bench)
For *Jimmy Long*
(Sacramento)

Itch-hour,
Itch hour in a courtroom warm with worry:
Where justice sometimes is courtjester/
Joker in a stacked deck;
Itch-hour, also, in a street-world,
Bitching-hour where truth is a color-couched nightmare:
        "Let my people Go!"
Itch-hour for steel-tongue warrior
Whose color is *handcuffs,* is *straitjacket,* is *cage*
From whose clutches he must stage trial,
Stage trial and community triumph:
        "Let my people Go!"
Bitching and stitching hour, bewitching hour,
For warrior! wishbringer! oracle! mojoMan!
Prophet of the larynx!
Peerless priest! Black pontiff in exile!
Wordwick and *wordspear;*
Itch-hour, again, and the ghetto gonggong is silent;
Silent in this place/in this joustroom
Where Blackmen caucus iridescent mouthmagic
To juju judges and jaw-frozen jurors:
Itching hour where mothers kneel or nod
And white bondsmen bargain;
Where hums flockfather and swordsworn troubador;
Caller, grandseer, summoner, sage and medicine-man:
Nat Turner, sunglassed, at the moaning bench;
Malcolm at the pearly gates;
Stokely stroking the River Jordan;

King, shoulderholstered, at the mountaintop:
>   *"Let my people Go!"*

Bookbrawn/based, lathered in blood, folk-supple
And songborne: folkseam and folksun:
>   *"Let my people Go!"*

TREK-SONG, MACK-SONG

For *James Baldwin*, *Ralph Ellison*, and *John Steinbeck*

Grapes of wrath, ground/danced into wine:
> / *"Drink wine, spodie-yodie, drink wine!"* /

Georgia-pine-high, America's *invisible man*
Stammers or performs stunts
In the country's viscera . . .
Is flushed through the anals
Of the national debt:
> / *"Drink wine, whale with them plucks!"* /

Trekking, trekking, trucking:
Hauling ass, marijuana, cocaine,
Hashish, heroin, LSD and much dick;
Trekking through Memphis, St.Louis,
MoTown, Cleveland, Philly, The Big Apple,
New Ark — — — — —
Macking across the Mohave Desert,
Riding thin rivers into Orange County, California,
Watutsi-ing through Watts and Compton;
Trucking / *"Express yo'self: in a hurry!"* /
Trekking, Macking on a conveyor belt moving to the rear:
> / *"Drink wine, my man"* /

Whaling, smoking, cooking, bucking, snorting:
> / *"Don't let the man make you turn no tricks, Jim!"* /

Runsong, beat-up-and-done song;
Ever-winning/ever-losing/ever-ebbing trektune.

STEELSONG IN STILLWATER

For *The Four Tops* and *"Smokey" Bill Robinson*

The penis of thought *upthrusts,*
Erects columns we must climb
To peer/prevail/above oppressive
Urine that *drowns* our gods
And *damns* our nostrils;
Downthrusts, sunray-steady,
To dagger deceptive surface waves . . .
To drill eye and mind into *yesterhorizons*
In stillest depth, with stoniest stare,
With sharpest song:
   "Deep river . . . my home is over Jordan"
To that level where water becomes lead stance,
Becomes stoic river of blues, becomes even sharper song,
Becomes ancestral gong steelsounding/stillpounding;
Thrusts to inject bloodjuices into deep heart of thought,
Steep backbone/spine-ladder of folkdreams, veins
Of visions and leathery feet of pilgrimage:
   "Deep river . . . my home is over Jordan"
Leathery feat of legend-building, leathery feet of lore;
Thrusts a remedy, Thrusts a melody, Thrusts a male-note:
   "Steel Waters Run Deep!"

HUMMIN', HOOKIN' & COOKIN'

"You got me hummin'"
For *Sam and Dave*

Bodies bloat the air
　　　　　/into an after-supper casserole/
Bodies sing /now/ and are *lovinglybruised*, brushed,
　　　　　Plaitted and pig-tailed
　　　　　On a shifting bed of coals;
Caringly battered and cured,
　　　　　Marinated in perfume, talcum powder
　　　　　/after-shave love/
Sauced, ensouled,
Saladed in unintelligible vowels
　　　　　colliding consonants/
In whispers, in hums, in hisses
　　　　　/through the bodies' alleys/
Through the sensuously uttering utensils/utonsils
　　　　　/baking and broiling/
In sweat, in tongue-tickling jawjuice;
Cookin' in pillow-cased ovens of ecstasy,
　　　　　/on sheet-covered thrill-grills/
Hookin' the meals of fulfeelment
Onto clothes-pin fingers,
Fingers that grip medium-rare rumps
Or welldone joypebbles glistening
On shores of liver-like skinskillets:
　　　　　/*succulent* and *surrealuscious*/
Peppery parting of a vaginal menu —
Hocks *hummin'* in fried sweat,
Boiling in sweat:
Need enunciated in beerflavored barbecue;

Body-cuisine scrumptiously offered:
/*fillet of desire*/   /souffle/
Stewed orgasms, groundbeef,
/milkwarm tongues on platters/
Fingerforks peeling back the fore-skin
Of brownbananas:
Bodies marinated, *lovingly bruised*,
Fried in sweat, in spit,
/lovingly bruised/
Talcum powder on medium rare muscles,
Lips sippin' lips,
Bodies marinated:
/*hummin'*/
/*hookin'*/
/*cookin'*/

BALLAD OF BLACK/ESSENCE

For *Joseph Harrison*

Firstforce or earth-driven godman; globe-song:
      Dance-embroidered in rhythmtree;
Flamefever inside blood, inside raindrops;
      Phono-song from a phono-sea.

Drumgirl, horizon-child: sprite moondancer!
      Fleshtorch, essence and *jewelskin*:
Comming/coming strongsong, blues-laced and black:
      Deftly making words out of wind.

Landlaced man, mud-docked and *waterwavy*,
      Oh *steel* that walks, that swims, that *flies!*
Softstone with armor to endure: to lure;
      Flowers inside iron: inside eyes!

Fleet/force, redemptive strength, precious muscle:
      Essence, the blackline and the core:
Beauty   /yes/   vim-vexed and *fire within fire*
      That *flares up!* frames and fans the shore:

That *flares up!* enflames the shore of seacoals;
      Giving and summoning the seed
Of light, sun, flamedances on rockshoulders:
      Burning and branding in our need;
      Burning and branding in our need.

CANE-BRAKE-BLUES

Remembering Jean Toomer's *Cane*

Got me some canebrake blues /baby/ this sugarpain sho is bad;
Got me some canebrake blues /baby/ this sugarpain sho is bad;
This sweet/sweet sore /man/ just keeps me happy-sad.

Cane blade cuts my mind / make my thoughts runred;
Cane blade cuts my mind / make my thoughts runred;
Cane dagger in my brain / knife-sweetenin' my head.

Cane crams wind down my throat / I'm hollerin from earth's hole;
Cane crams wind down my throat / I'm hollerin from earth's hole;
Sounds just symphonizing / resurrecting my old, old soul.

Got some canebrake blues, sweet/mama,
Got some canbrake blues
Got some canbrake blues, sweet/mama,
          /got some canebrake blues/
But with this sugarpain power
How can I lose
How can I lose
How can I lose . . . .

SHARPEVILLE STING/SONG

For *Oliver Jackson*, Painter,
After *"Sharpeville Series"*

Mechanical sharpshooters
      /villains/
Reload lightning sticks
That mutter/sputter harsh sparklanguage
At hungryflesh huddled in the streets;
Sharpeville Song, Sharpeville Symphony
Harpoons through bodies, slaughter-house bunched,
Sagging from blood-dirt dampness,
Lagging behind life   /given up to lore/
To folkgossip and handlers of decaying human decor.

Sharpshooters singing   /now/   from pompous books:
Word-barrages   /automatic elocutionists/   sugarfill the fleshholes;
Journalists and Jurists trotting
/In high-breed grace/   across conscience courts,
Pantomiming gods/ghouls and meandering in mouthwash.

Sharpeville knowing   /now/   that ancestral bowmen
Will blow-dart a deed-for-deed vengeance;
That underneath trees juju-ers sing sharpwrath:
As Sharpevillains chop at natal cords
        /try to brake birthing nationhood/
With swords of technology   /mindless slashes/
With knives of false knowledge:
Sharpeville sting rings in earthbelly
For BlackJustice; for redemption of
Unprovoked suffering, of *UnAskedFor* death.

SONNET SERENADE/SOULO BEAUTY

For *Gwendolyn Brooks*

Behold! the forms and rhythms of my face:
Choral trees and soulos limbly bowing;
Greenhiss/grasslow and moanful in sparkspace,
Caught cyring/caroling and know-howing;
Sometimes in gusty *soulsoliloquys*
Within vastvalleys and mountainous songs;
Or much/iterated with ah's and me's,
Short/circuited or shattered against gongs.

A lord-length voice invades these jungles sparks:
Neoning/drumscripting a passion-rain
Which seeds tear-tunes and in the drumpath marks:
A cool/mellow maid of song and a main
Squeeze close-held in sound-arms, in hip song-rap;
Whose love, buttoned in gold, is your lyre-lap.

MOOD-AFRO/FIRE

Thinking of *"Duke"* and *"Mood Indigo"*

From a spiritual quiver
Soars an ache/ an arrow;
Comes steel spines, holy hypodermics, rich marrows;
Comes boiling boneJuice we drink
       /fluid-triggered thoughts/
BoneJuice we inject into trees for safe-keeping;
/Mood Afro/   keepsakes trance-clasped in trees/
Knuckle-rooted in *jewelrock*, in fatherground;
Dance-dark clefs cuddled/huddled
Readied in bowstrong across hearth, across heart,
Unleashed in rhymes of time, of tart:
       of *Elegance!*
       of *Poetrees!*
       of *DanceBodies!*
       of *Bloodstones!*
       of *Jewelrock!*
When the neck is nailstiff
With the virus of oppression,
With the virus of mis-history:
Mood Indigo is a cadence-test of fire,
Of *BluesFlame:* Mood Afro,
The midwife of the moon,
Blackblanket and electric quilt
Close-circuiting a furled world,
Circling a world with quiver
       /spirit current/
A shiver of harmony, of bone/hardharmony:
       of *ElegantPoetrees!*
       of *DanceBodies in Bloodstones!*
       of *Jewelrock!*

HAPPENIN' HARMONY

For *Marvin Gaye, Curtis Mayfield & Margaret Walker*

We are voice-lifted people/
/elevators humming suns/
Syncopating profound noise: people of . . .
/Garrulous pride/
Purple grace
". . . bloody peace . . ."/
Quiet moonmurmuring devotion;
Blackbalanced soilfooted
/darker than pre-creation hollowness/
Lighter than the WORD,
Faithfull as fertility symbols/silent temptresses
In ageless voice-tapestries: *and ancienter!*
Africanbones bledred through treebark arms.

"Moving on up!" a starphonic scale
/and across HOW MANY river!/
Along roadblades and knife-notes,
Moving to the bluesgloom of God,
The bluesgroom of a *Lady Day Like Goddess;*
The people of knuckle-wrought calm;
Of dimple-clad, riddle-bad, melodies;
Of intonated ecstasy:
"What's happenin', brother?"
The people yesterspirits serenade
With parables/preachments transported
In the wombvoice of the wind:
"What's happenin', brother?"
"What's happenin', sister?"

SOUTHERN SOUND:
A BROODING UNDER BLOOD

For *Charles Rowell*, after summer, 1971,
Baton Rouge, Louisiana

Creole, collard greens
And hoodoo hymns against a gumbo sky —
> *"Soil song*
> *Spoil song"*

Dixie chant is Black road to *steelhammermountain*
DeepSouth ritual is discreet strength,
Darklore is harpdance in a lyricfield —
> *"Spoil song*
> *Soil song"*

Fatback, hogjowls and juju
And the mind is farmland/is swarmland
For this newnation in embryo,
For this bee-busy commotion
And earthward polychatter —
> *"Soil song*
> *Spoil song"*

Bloodland, blooddocks and bloodfruit
And a child, ripe;
And a mind, ripe: ripe with sting or strut
Like sugarblades of cane
Or louisiana browngirls whose passions
Gestate in volcanos,
Hesitate under quiet cotton colors —
> *"Spoil song*
> *Soil song"*

Dixie Chorus is an African call/
Watutsi-tall, *greening with upsongs*
Hoodoo hymns in a lyricfield
Against a gumbo sky.

DANCE BODIES #1

Spitfire! from *BlackFleshMotors*
          /whirhums/
Under acrobatic howls:
Zig-grip! Zig-grip! Zig-grip!
Zag-lore! and bodies brush air;
Dip-twist! Down-bend! Dip-twist!
And kissing palms pancake/applaud air,
Chop smoke/humpsreams:
JamesBrowning the breakdown!
BrakeDowning the JamesBrown!
Washing air with sugarsweat/
With antiseptic potion and polish;
Caroling *fleshmotors* flinging/
Ringing from shirt or skirt:
          "Boogaloo on through!
          Breakdown the walls, brother!
          Boogaloo on through!"
Footfire on floor of hot coals:
Split! Get up! Toe turn!
          /Split!/ /Toe-turn!/
Heel-tunes screeching:
          "Bank-here! Break-there!"
Kissing palms pancake/paralyze the air:
Sugarsweat sterilizing air
With gymnastic intelligence/
With braindance acrobatics/
With spitfire from *fleshmotors* — humming:
          "Boogaloo on through!
          Breakdown the walls, brother!
          Boogaloo on through!"

LYRICS FOR LEON

For *Leon Thomas* and "Spirits Known and Unknown"

> *songstitch to mend*
> *songstitch to mend*

Encoding a cry, a call, a blues-epic
     /turning song into corduroy sky/
You birth a feathery voice/scream!
Airborne in ridges of an African overcast:
Brick-throated balladeer!
Decoding hieroglyphics in the groin,
In the script of ancient drumvoices —
> *songstitch to mend*
> *songstitch to mend*

"Leaping Leon": erupting into rhapsodic mountains:
> *"oola-boo oola-boo oola-boo*
> *oola-boo oola-boo oola-boo*
> *oola-oola oola-oola oola-oola*
> *oodle-ee boo-ee oodle-ee boo-ee*
> *oodle-la-boo oodle-la-boo"*

Torchnotes! Flame-throat!
Raging in phonic forests
     /tree-tunes/
In fireblades that chop and copper-crust
The corduroy sky of song —
> *songstitch to mend*
> *songstitch to mend*

Soulo- and echo-child, seedspring of sound
Eloping, groping,
With demons of coastal storms/
Noiseless mistresses of docks and deserts:
Riverrhythm, exorcising *spirits known and unknown,*
Moving up/down ladders of sunstreams;
Chorusing/caressing stars, making tones galactic,
Orchestrating initial buzzes and bums:
> *songstitch to mend*
> *songstitch to mend*

TUNE FOR A TEENAGE NIECE

For *Jeanine Spencer*

Smile/rippling river of dance —
Flow, blow green soul-lyre
Ballooning under brown flesh:
Song/swirl, startling as claps
Of unexpected waves;
Girlriver dancing its drumdeep past,
Its boogalooborn/e day,
Fluteflown afro freight
*Grand*mother/mamma/aunt — sun-led —
Yesterwhistling confluence
          /childwoman and charmsong:
          "Brown blues and honey-river, girl!
          Blues-brown and river-honey, girl!
          Girlmother gonna sing her song someday, boy!
          Brown blues and honey-river, girl!"
Smile/river dancing, splashing flame-waves
Applaud and burn/mold *brownfruit*,
Afro-plum,
River symphony, water ritual:
          "Brown blues and honey-river, girl!"
Girlriver, spiced as pot liquor, flowing up/under
From queenmother's heartbeam; from magic and marmelade;
Fluteflown to fleshdance and birdgrace:
Flowing to *omen*, to *woman:*
          "Brown blues and honey-river, girl!"

SOUND OF A HEART-TRAIN

For *John Coltrane* & *Johnny Hartman*
(Impulse Stereo LP: -40)

Twice/together:
Two rails of ache hurtle this groupheart
Rails — ailings — of sound moaning, honing stone paths
                    /*Stone lone*/
Bleeding and balladeering a dignity of stresses;
Tracks criss-crossing a scale of time and tones;
Making *fancydance* the ear
                    /polylayered the movement, *the lyric:*
                    /lumbersome *the love;*

Beneath rails, between rails
Daring drumheart arches a crescendo of thumps and thunder,
Bumps and hums: a cardiacting rhythm section,
Drumbass, for rails of sound, for ails of sound,
Soaring! Exploring!
            Horned voice!
            Brassflesh and rail!
            Cocaine, sometimes, and tail!
Powdered blood blown/thickened to stone
To tracks of steelrhyme:
Shuttling invisible cargo, indivisible cargo,
The *weight*, the *worry*, the *freight*, the *fret*,
The goldenstool of stereo tucked in/under
In/under rails of ache hurtling this groupheart:
            Horned voice!
            Brassflesh and rail!
            Cocaine, sometimes, and tail!

KIN-NOTE

For *Jim & Lindell Penn*
Sacramento, California

Bloodlinks lug each Sunday towards summer;
Bloodphones upspirit/amplify soup of smalltalk
With feasts of *royalblack rap;*
And sandwiches of chatter
Orchestrate humming rain, make drumfeetchant,
Milk faces to flow   /overflow/
In *riverlivingroom*
Where fireplace frets or cackles henlike;
And minds, wobbled by weeklong wars,
Are propped up, to unwind, in carpet crevices:
This is /after all/ "yall"
A caucus of Black gall,
A gut-gathering,
A visceral bridge nataling hallelujah spirts:
Hamhocking Sunday into a slumber of soundlore
Sirloining summer into a latch of love
In whose belly autumn fertilizes/rainbows/laughlores
A soultree of kinfriends.

IN THE FLESHFLAME THAT IS HER FACE

In the fleshflame that is her face,
The fire burns her clearer to me;
And in her apricot ears, the stereophonic
Flames lick and crack, playing playing
Back the sounds of teeth roasting in gumgreases.

In the fleshflame that is her face,
The nose is an anvil of leavening:
A symmetrical center, a symmetrical song
Of two hollows bleeding the air with
Their silent drum-operas.

In the fleshflame of her face
Lie launch pads for eye-rockets,
Two springboards of sight stalking
And reaching the rims of things —
For eyes reach further than arms.

Oh flameflares that are her eyes!
Oh fireflies that are her eyes!

In the fleshflame of her face
Old urges and urns burn: Plenipotentiary
Pyres of the past watching over
This charred-copper queen:

The flash/flame that is her face,
The force that is her fire,
The flame that is her fight,
The fuse that is her light,
Is the fleshflame of her face!

IN A TIME OF RAIN
& DESIRE

BOYJEWEL: DAZZLE-MAN

For Godson *Ross Mark Williams*,
born April 12, 1973: 8:15 a.m.

New Blink in the world —
Coiled fleshsong, *Marking* time,
In the crib of caress —
On the incline of love:
     Hey hey boybloom!
     Hey hey manflower!
     Hey hey songbud!
Nightsong, spice-wind in the world —
Blues coil, fleshknot, on the tree of man,
In the sun's constant veil —
In the high hovel of special grace:
     Hey hey boybloom!
     Hey hey mandance!
Manfret unfurling toward every-which-away —
Manseed, planting muscles in Chicago-ground:
     Hey hey boybloom!
     Hey hey manbud!
     Hey hey tree-tune!
Swirlcry, acrobat in coil, blinking prince —
Totemic majesty, *watch watch watch* the world open!:
Watch watch watch, dig!, the world open!
But stretch but coil but sing but watch!
     Hey hey boytree!
     Hey hey Afro-fidget!
     Hey hey boybloom!
     Hey hey!
     Hey hey!
     Hey hey!

LIGHT UNSHRUNKEN

There is a light —
     quiet beam of brotherlore —
A searing sunfire of sistergleam/
Fragrant sheen of contemporary struggle;
A corridor /changed from cave to palace:
     dim-cave to Black-palace/
There is a light /some sun crouching in a rock/
A love-light shouldered against a new slavery,
Slinging a new freedom song from the Davids of our day:
Seeing love /deathless love/
Seeing effort /deathless effort/
A light that crushes
Night into small glitter-gardens where suns grow
And girlstars gestate.
They can't take it away —
Even in the flicker,
The stumble,
The fire of upstance will flare again:
Our light,
Fist-motored love, flame-powered love,
A passion unshrunken.

MAIN MAN BLUES

Do you know my
Slap-a-hand, lend-a-hand main man?

Dirt-deep podner,
Quick-reeling, nigger-feeling friend, then?

Knife-blocker,
Vagina stopper,
Wit-knitted — not-to-be-shitted — bad man?

Have you ever had the *main man blues?*
Have you ever re-dug or coat-tailed
That cleanfully nasty harbinger of corner cuss?

Brothergone/Brother-coming?
Spitfire well digger
Who never got no bigger?
That ghetto-phonic nigger?

In the streets, on the sheets — where we sopped up our own blood;
In the churches — where we prayed, preyed, squinting
At fat old sisters or plumb-luscious classmates?

Brothergone/Brother-coming?
Hot rags macker, righteous!
Hot cock tracker, righteous!
Bigdaddy, uncle of mercy in the git-down times:
Slap-a-hand, lend-a-hand, main man?

POSTSCRIPT

At 2 am this morning
        I awoke
2 am webbed in a wrinkled geography of sheets
        I awoke
To see your hands ploughing your hair
Your body an incompleted *S*
In fetus-like tranquillity,
Cocooned in the port of your last orgasm;

With throttle open, I thought:
        You always swell so-quickly
        And I grow to contain, refrain you:
        Yet, like a tree, you branch and branch
        In the forest of my multiplying hungers;
        Or, like a balloon, in puberty, you gasp
        And burst — gasp and burst:

At 2 am your rage is a timid whir: otherwise, othering:
And I wonder what voodoo vassal shrank you so?
What manner of God forested your fruits and,
At 2 am, shrinks and calms your fire into the crook of my arm?

O! WHERE HAS NIGHT FLOWN? O!

Interplanetary lady:

Between whose legs the moon languishes:
And, in embryo, the dew-braided sun
Sizzles in another region of your galaxy;
And my need growing to gluttonous fever —
Which your clasp circumferences with cool bars of passion;
And my muscular tranquilizer is a tower:
>   O arched bomb of jelly!
>   O balm for ails and itches
>   And lacerations between your legs —
>   Where night sleeps with leopards
>   Where night pants like a race-dog
>   Where night throbs like a laundromat:
>   Becomes magic wand to ward off day,
>   To keep the dark lid on this room of ecstasy;

Not that my love cannot thrive on sunlight
>   /for our eyes are suns/
But for the sake of blue flames
Burning in an orange warmth
Aboard the moon in you — O long gone night!
O morning when, again, we meet our oppressors!
O morning when we meet our forefathers' makers!
O mourning where the Armageddon of orgasms unhums in
>   sunstrokes!
O mourning when the second-coming is the last coming —
>   and then none!
O mourning when dew is all that's left of our night-lit orgy!
O morning, O daybreak; O night-breaking wind in the mouth
>   of morning!

O morning! O slithers through the blinds of night!
O drapes fallen from the hinges of the dark!
O all my needs and flanks telescoped by the sun!
O woman-length vortex for the vibrations of my heats!
O woman-length maelstrom for the relics of my passion!
O museum! O tapestry and mural and subterranean self!
O submarine-of-a-woman twirling in Ocean-I!
        in Sea-I!
        in river-I!
O where has night flown/
        With its nostrils of dark air?
        With its electric landscapes?
        With its comings-and-goings / comings-and-goings?
And O! how much darkness can you hold in your hand?
And O! how much darkness can we belly-grip between us?
And O! how much darkness can an idea contain?
And O! what is the weight of darkness?
And O! how long /yes, how long/ is darkness?
And O! how dark is need; how many days make up a second
    of sorrow?

And O! O! where has the night flown!
With you, and the moon, between your legs?

LADY: A LOVE NAMED FREEDOM

Last night
I crept from my cage of color
/the prison of my past/
And made love
To a lady named *Freedom;*
She was countless
And, almost, mountless — but I made it!
Made her:
Achieved that voluptuous summit,
Then rode her vertical luxury:
Her jewelry-laden lap of pain
Into the valley of mirrors
/valley of echoes/
Into the dry mouth of night
Into the arms of Freedom
/an armless woman/
Where I, in birthday nakedness,
Diluted my chant with prayer:
Where the wind made of me a rocking-chair
/back-and-forth: back-and-forth/;
Miss Freedom, in a gown of flesh,
Stretched out, straddled me in her armlessly abandoned passion:
>*And Aretha appeared in Goddess-Glare*
>*And Angela came as Lordess of Love*
>*Roberta with "quiet-fire" to scorch me on, on*
>*Sojourner appearing with a proclamation of my manhood*
And Lady Freedom softening to a night
Of feminine opportunity:
A cavern of Blacklites I enter
To find my brain erecting

Inside a web of *blood-lines*
Inside a fire of *newyouth* —
Inside a flame that licks my testicles
And tells me to leap to the roof
Of Chance and mount the charcoal queen
Shaken from kitchen sleep —
Belly-dancing her way out of shackles!

Last night I crept
Crept from the cage of my color,
Made love to a Lady named Freedom:
Incestuously succumbed to my siamese twin,
My brother known as night;
Last night I left the cage of color,
The mystique of my hue,
And retraced the rainbow
For the whereabouts of God.

NOT REJECTION:BUT COMPLEX AND PAINFUL TRUTH

I cannot solve the riddle of your needs
Nor salve the cerebral pricking of your pain;

You cannot solve the silence of my chill
Nor what you see as sadism in my thrill
            /the strange night-air passing between us/
/shuddering our bodies & shifting our allegiances/
You say I owe you the luxury of a lie
            /that I should stay!/
You say worry is the flipside of ecstasy
I say worry is the midwife of life
            /O decisions!/
And through the same door love enters and exits
And through the same door passes game and blame
            /O decisions!/
But love is not a baton in a relay race:
Neither a nugget nor a broach
            /And how can I return what I never received?/
And if I could give you dividends on your love
How could I repay God for breath?
            /O decisions!/
And chances;
I take chances in the whirlwind
            /in the laundromats of change/
On the washingboards of life —
To be give-less is not rejection:
But, complex and painful truth.

LOVE IS NOT A WORD

Do not ensnarl me in a sphere of nouns
Nor cage me in a lair of adjectives:
My need is no funeral song for freedom —
My heat is not electronic:

Do not calibrate my sun with thermometers
Nor pierce my "secret parts" with telescopes:
My cause is not a tableau of codes —
My cry is not stereophonic:

Do not titillate the totem of my thought
Nor advertise, on open market, my privacy:
My rampant passion is not a freak for laboratories —
My pain is not catatonic:

Do not ring me with monotonous vows
Nor sting me with laconic lectures, with commands:
My need is not a force to fence in —
My itch is not metronomic:

Do not label me with foreign lore
Do not place this epiphany in frames
Do not lock my indivisible rhythm in names
Do not color-in my pageless, endless book
Do not describe my dialog with trees
Nor transcribe what the moon whispers
Do not record the voice in my eyes:
Yet *look look look look*, and
Don't dismiss me as a synonym for love.

HEART-WOUNDS DO NOT HEAL

For asylum from such wounds
There is always a scab:
            /some mascara/
Sunglasses for flooding wells in the face
            /laughter/
Withdrawalism or anonymous liquids in a glass
            /humor/
Laces or silks or high-hats
            /excuses/
A new surge: a new risk: a new squeeze
            /vanity/
An analysis, a tear-length night, resoluteness
            /indulgence/
Long sleeves for clawed flesh, for itch-marks
            /wherewithal/
And night dawns a mirror of daylight
On the immediacy of the mind
            /worry/
And, again, the reflection is actual
            /a sigh refracted in screams/
            /and a ballistics test says the tears came from blood/
Where the bed is a cage in which to wrestle with night
Or be still and listen to the gasping of the dark
Or the heart   /wounded and wounded and wounded/
Which will not *heal*
And the ghosts you cannot kill!

BARBED WIRE LOVE

It is not from a lust
For pain
That I press against the barbed wires
Of phantom love:
Or lure my people's need
Onto the flickering
Shores of my privacy
When I know the calculating
Waters of heathens are threatening flood;

It is not from fondness
For defeat that I
Go again and again
Into hybrid vineyards
Of America's conscience
Or the open-eyed icicle-gloom
Of my people's amnesia —
For love is an inner drum
For love is an inner drum;

It is not to the suicidal call
Of skyscraper gods
That I fasten My future
          /stake all my mornings/
On the inner-star of struggle
          inner-star of struggle
That beacon sparked by voices
Of my father's gods against
The flintstones of night —
For love is not an iridescent limousine
To ride in:

But, some say,
A chariot of darts
That fidgets in wounds
Opened daily like windows to the sun —
But often, some say,
The clasp, by toes,
Of tightwires above the market place

Where flesh is a bestseller
And love is lobotomized —
Where flesh sizzles
And love glints and gropes.

LOVE AS UPBRINGING

Where the willows drag the ground
And coal sheds
Slant tar-paper heads
Towards ring-wormed sunflower stalks,
My love grew
From a seed
Draped in a tear poised in my grand/mother's eye —
In East St. Louis,
In the saintlessness of slot-machines
In the ring of gunfire
In the cackle of hussies:
In beneath-the-bridge taverns
My boyhood notions
Were nudged, made adventurous,
By the pipe-puckered/snuff-stained
Lips of teethless troubadors —
Strumming/strumming
Out their blemishes and boasts:
On gatemouth guitars and widowed washing boards —
In the *southend* with the roar of trains
Rushing through Rush City:
A crater,
A scowl of agony
On the face of a land
Saddled by the bridges of whitemen:
Bridges whose tracks   /screeching & screeching/
Were long-play records fused from the fossils of Blackmen:
O the melody of freight!
In Beulahland
Where the dead died, often, at home
And the coffins lay open

In doily-decorated livingrooms:
My love, my hunger for chainless manhood upsoared!
In the shacks of my mind
In the vision of cotton-dresses
In my tattered totems of hope
My grandwise grandmother
My love grew from blisters
My love grew from sore rumps
My love outlined against the gutter-grim sunken streets
Against
The geniuses nodding
In unlabeled bottles.

LITTLE LOVES: SAVE THEM

Little boy
Little girl

Glued to the sole
And a hip-shaking God —
Oozing
Oozing
Bumping bopping buzzing
On the clouds of my hopes
Glowing in incinerators of the city
Glowing in *legitimized* tombs
Of urban mummies
Oozing
Joy joy trapped in carbon-tarted air:
Little seeds
From which Black caravans grow
From which our gloom is lifted
On which our personal dooms are defied:
As Marvin Gaye says,
Save them.

IN LOVE, IN TERROR

Outside the huddle
Of maniacs
And the rapid-fire political rhetoric
Grows a love-bud,
A flesh-sappling
Reaching toward tree-hood
In sandy air —
A Blackboy a Brownboy,
In a land unpromised:
Blooming from a drop of blood
Left in the night of woman;
A love-bud
Stretching past a wall
That boards up justice
And hugs the napalmed night:
Toward tree-hood grows
This princely lyric,
This love-bud,
This Blackboy Brownboy,
This nightlad king-that-was/king-could-be
Whose body is a nation-seed
Whose body is a flame
Enveloping the dark.

TO LOVERS, BLACK & WHITE

Until you de-penis
Your brain, Blackman
        /cease to pantomime the passionate
         correctness of your fathers/
You can love
Neither Black nor White Woman.

Until you harden the jelly of your back, Whiteman
        /lace it with the super-spine of truth/
Until you deflate
The balloon of your phantom history /fear of Black Phallus/
You can love
Neither White nor Black Woman.

I CAN NEVER UNLOVE YOU

To *not want*
Is to *not exist*
Is to be de-minded
Is to be disembodied
Is to be disem-personed
And float like an apparition
Into the non-where
Into the grey whim of limbo
And that is why I can never unlove you:
      why I can never dismantle my passion
      why I can never decompose my desire

To reel in my cautious need:
Is to be unclumsy in hyperposture
Is to be a cursed garden, growthless
Is to be made breathless by outside strictures
And nod in noon-sun like
A drunken lizard —
A slitherless drip on the echo of love
      on the back of some nomadic breeze
      on the coattail of sanity
And that is why I can never unlove you
      why I can never unnotice the flames you forge
      why I can never unloose my eyes from their aim

I can never unlove you
Though I can re-love you before another moon
I can never un-need you
Though I can re-grieve the night-stained caresses
I can never not want you
Though I can re-cry the ancientest ocean:
I can never unlove you:
Unlove you . . .
Never.

MIDWAY IN THE NIGHT: BLACKMAN

Blackman
    /midway in the night/
In the Beulahland of cabarets
       /bronco-busting the moon/
Silent is the howl, hung & mouth-held —
Your penis wrapped, rope-like,
Round your neck:
Your penis clotted, knot-like,
At your throat:

Your manhood dog-loosed
On the auction block
Of an American whim:
Your love cluttered with white fear
Your womanview hazed by the rat-tat-tat
Of assassins who snipe your future
And ambush your history:
Black man,
Lover man:
Man of much-dick
Night-fuck hero
Quick-love artist
Dashman —
Don't let your penis protrude, goat-horn-like,
Through your skull:
Butting its way through
The tender muscular enclosures of your woman:
So anxious you cannot take the last shirt
Off the back of your mind:
So driven you cannot
Utter, in low register / in timed-tone,

BLUES: 'GIMME' IS A WOMAN, PRAISE JESUS!

Gimme, yes! is *she-fire*
   /charcoaling my mind/
With lips lured from the mother-sure past,
     the African vast;

Gimme didn't get drowned!
Gimme didn't get drowned!
Gimme got rounded,
     mounded,
By the fever-spear of my father;

Mother-munch woman, *Gimme*,
With hot hot dampness
To boil daddylong, daddylong
    like shadows
    like thighs;
Daddylong that trickles
    that runs/
Gimme, girl! is *she-fire* —
Boil-of-a-woman, kneck-bone-nubber:
The delicate opening of her mother's gush
   /and I, I the measure of my father's rush/
Gimme, then, is *she-fire* sweating the flare that erects me,
Glistening in churchroar
   /sinners beware!/
Pious in the burning pew, Angelic in sweets —
   and devil on the sheets:
Gimme, Lord!, is *she-fire!*

NIGHT IN LIQUID

Liquid-filled night,
Fleshfilled moon:
  And I, wine-watered manflower:
   wine-flower, manwatered;
  And you, bourbon-bloomed girlbush:
   bushgirl, bourbon-bloomed;

Passion circle in a square /in triangle/
Immaculate transfusion!
Spontaneous poles of ecstasy!
  And I, love, loomed in the dark:
   helicoptering above you/
   rotating into your cavernous climates;
Moored in the effortless night
  /day wombed in our expectancy/
  /day drizzling down on us/
Morning anointing girlbush, manflower;
  And you, stretching like Himalayas before me/
   unfoldingly spiced by my sweat, my squirm;
  And you, forest;
  And you, river;
  And you, ensemble of the landscape /of the joyscape/;
A crescendo of limbs and tunes catching fire,
Burning into damp heat of wombvision,
Burning into flesh coals of nightgored woman:
Where we sweat and swear
  sweat I swear
  sweat and swear . . .

SHE WALKS IN A CIRCLE OF AIR

She walks in a circle of air
(the evening snores around her) —
She walks in a circle of air
Into a nodding night
/O boundaryless drape!/
/O corridor of dust!/

Into an indivisible darkness:
Into the moon
Where a green guitar
Strums/struts to join the lyricism
That hums my wants
That hounds my wounds
/O never to be obliterated love!/

This quicksand of my desire
Where all swirls & furls   /proud sails/
Gather to stealbirth the day
(and the blanket that seals off the sun
flaps like a headless chicken);
And my need is a spinning
Nomad with watery fingers
On the desert of her body —
Around which whirls the
Quiet cough of God —
Around which whirls and whirls the maddened meteors
(the envious eyes that fall from wooden faces) —
And she walks in a circle of air.

NIGHT LOVE: POSTSCRIPT

Dry rings of love. Lull.
Sheets rippled rolled. Ridges. Horizons of the bed.
        /stillwaves of clothe/
Your legs listless plows. Bone-fled flesh.
In a fleshgarden
Orgasms grow. Sensual insignia.
Music. Night search. Liquid neon
Morning. Chill vault quiver.
First yawn of day.
Trees shudder. Showers for the mat of dawn.
Sun blinks. Sun bleats.
Dry rings of love. Love is a bedwetter.
Saliva on your thighs: Damballah's inscription.
Lust of last night: nude-scrawled bed-rings.
Hissdrone of shower. Bathroom giggle, gurgle, gurgle.
Marvin Gaye's moan: *"Trouble Man" Trouble.*
Trouble:
        /*nobody* knows de trubble I be . . ./
Sun tears. Shower hissdrone. Your
Thighs cry: cringe from the sun's hexing eye.
Night shrinks back into your woods. Night shrinks.
Shrinks back into the womb of God.

A CANDLE OF STRUGGLE LIGHTS THE ROAD

Around me
       /within me/.
The greatest love   /"no greater love"/
Flourishes & frets:
This struggle is a sharp
Point on the dial of my momentum
         /sharp point/
— that jabs jabs away at my
Intestinal freedomtude
Where oppression is a reality,
Blunt as a dream:
Around me
        /within me/
My brethren boil
And are cooked in open ovens of humiliation
Or pierced by needle-point
Or jailed by irridescent stripes & weaves
Or silenced by remute control of tv —
In me
        /around me/.
The candle of struggle scorches the road
And burns for me; burns me:
Consumes me, sometimes,
In petite objectives
        And my people on the stilts of materialism!
        And my brothers doing about-faces
        Before foreign gods —
It is a love weighty & war-lured
A come-late

A rise-early pain
                    Where a circle of boasts
                    Where a circle of threats
                    Cloaks the obsolesence of freedom fighters
                    Cloaks the desperation of daddies:
Where poets move moorless & craftless
To the temporary stars of prefabricated thrones
                    /false thrones for false poets/
To love in all the clutter, Lord?
To love in all the clutter?

And the struggle is a constant cross:
Humming injustice against thorns unseen;
And color is my strength
And color is my nation
And color is an albatross around the ghetto's neck!

The greatest love flourishes, frets
My struggle/
And always always there is the sweet
Suburban urge to landscape the secret tears:
To paper the walls of agony with greenbacks:
To hurtle through my people's mire
In block-long pimpmobiles:
                    /o temptation o temptation!/
Frothing love: this struggle a siren
Announcing that my guts have turned
To leather for the longfight:
Announcing that love is ambivalent armor:
A sword to fight with . . .
Or fall on.

SWEET LADY

Your torso an accordion
In my hands:
Hissing sighing humming
A divine stress and vigor;
Your limbs guitar strings
And I am your amplifier
And I am your amplifier:
Sweetlady,
It is not your sugar sagging;
But lemon-tarted honey
From which you unfurl and unfurl
From hymen-sealed girl
To plush furniture of woman
To open quicksands of passion:
Sweetlady,
Ripe with the fruit smell of life —
Ripe like the aromas entering/leaving you;
Sweet like the pain of need
Or the highhearted paranoia of anticipation;
When you come,
Filtering the sting of ammonia in my nostrils,
The taste of sweet-sour woman in my mouth,
The throb of hot-ice in my undergrowth:
Lady!

I KNOW THE STIGMA

I know the stigma
          /attached to the guitar between my legs/
That sucks the Blackman
Into the driftwood of nonchalance
Where love is a lump in his throat
Where love is a fear
Forming premature stains in his eyes —
The stigma that seduces his manhood
And sets him sail
On jealous waters of America's fantasy
The stigma impaled on his penis
          /o bronze muscle/
And jutting through the tempestuous
Nights of American dreams:
Jutting — as charismatic skyscraper
That whitemen ponder
And whitewomen cuddle:
A spermato-seed in the garden of European mythos.

I know the opulence of white wombs
Into which the Blackman's mind
Sometimes falls —
I know the stigma of the vaginal cage
Where freedom writhes in eternal fetus
Where the embryo of Blacklove
Shrinks from the light of grownup needs:
          /the unconfirmed reports/
I know the power of the fetish that dangles
Or coils between my legs
And hisses uncomfortably outside stud factories:

I know the sub-gods of my body
And the lore-ladened jewels
That are not the heirlooms of America:

I know the stigmas
            Even as Africa sees/oozes through me
            Even as my woman waits in the night
The stigmas that cauterize my care
The stigmas my father shrank from
The stigmas that taunt/tame America
The colossus I must fight
Lest I remain a nomad
On the endless body of the Black woman.

MY TONGUE PAINTS A PATH

My tongue paints a path of fire
Across her body
My tongue trickles unseen
And indelible tracks
Through the center of her metropolis —
As a flameless torch,
I burn beyond the color
Of heat into infinite fire:
Where her passion
Is onelong sigh of molten air
That my tongue
Banks to a burnsong:
Against the anvil of her geography:
That my tongue *rings* —
Where my tongue plunges plunges
Into the waters of her country —
Into the ravines,
The crops,
Of her forests.

INSIDE MY PERIMETER

Inside my perimeter
Of fears
A unit of guerillas
Strikes at the barbed-wired
Hovels that hoard our love:
That incarcerate our needs —
An insurgent army
Storms the bastille of pride,
Shells this façade of custom,
Knells the collapse
Of the straw men inside us —
Accepts the sun,
Allows the contorted face of
Stress to smile again —
To glow again!
Allows Love to Live.

MEDALS OF THE HEART

A highly decorated soldier
In the struggle for love,
He bumpwalks on the avenue:
Wearing bracelets strung from hearts
And beaded in the solitary
Tears of women —
His own pain pushed
Back so far into his fear
You cannot see
The dry blood of hurt
Used to blunt his swollen pyramid of bitterness
Used to tom-tom the sting of his memory
Used to stem the tide-waters
Of his bloated agony.

LOVE AS GNAW

Unknot the gnaw
That chokes
My testimony
And pumps worn tears
From a blues-bruised well of need:
I want to bear witness —
Love is trepidation
Love is an intestinal fire over-raging
                            over-burning
Love is a night-itch;
The skin-stains, the fidget,
The scars scorched by the noose of non-commitment
                            by the fingernails
That claw the fragile purr of worry:
Way way down into unslept slumber
When amnesia will not crowd
Out the curse
        /or conscience/
I want to bear witness —
Love is trepidation:
Varicose veins of worry —
Love is trepidation:
A clumsy clot that fist-thuds
In the mute caverns
Of need:
Witness, *Love is Trepidation!*

RAIN DESIRE RAIN DESIRE

Rain, desire
Desire, rain —
Joy-waters rise,
Fall;

Joy-waters leap,
Clap hands, roar through our abundance:
And the sky drips a sonorous tear
To my body contorted between your pillars
        /golden pillars/
My body weeping upon hilly thighs
And the fleshdoor of your lyrical corridor
Salved by sweat, by blood:
By rain
By desire
And I exit through a dawn that blares the chatter
Of artificial mornings; that drops a drape
Of light over the world's window
        over the dark torches we bear
        over our limb-lore
And the night rides an elevator
From the oasis of our ecstasies to the storehouse
Of rememberance: of relish:
Where rain hammers out memory
And the ghost of desire
Slips through wet thoughts:
Tiptoes on the damp dots of anxiousness:
                        of shiny climaxes.

REQUEST (IF IT'S NOT ASKING TOO MUCH)

Long for me,
Baby,
Anchor me deep within
Your within,
Lodge my presence between
Your thoughts,
Let me alternate with your
Breathing,
Discriminate in my favor,
Labor late in my cause,
Go through changes with me!
Fashion your heart into a pen
Dipped in your blood and bleach/brand
My name into the sky,
Rise rise up against those
Who put bad mouth on me!

Stand! stand! Mama!
Stand still
And wait relentlessly.
Be there!
Be there!
Be there!

MADSTING

More than ever, now,
I search for the switch of your nightbulb
      /rite bulb/
Sunken or elevated
In the moody mischief of bonelessness;
Wanting to fling my fermenting flesh
Upon the tortuous luminescence
Of your blacklite —
Needing to cram my need
Into the unnavigated crevices
And shadowed unexpectancies
Of your sprawlglare
        /I wanna make you shine!
         I wanna let you shine!/
Your madsting,
Your *stone*; into the gnomic provinces
        /I need to go!/
Where you murmurously vivisect
The catacombs of my love —
Where you stroke and straddle
My tubular slope, my genealogical garden,
My songbleeding scepter:
As the walls, sung-stiff by your litany,
Are jewel-oozed,
Jewel-oozed and collapse-less.

ON / AGAIN; OFF / AGAIN

This love/
    fastened to a lore of pain
        handcuffed to an indignity of ecstasy/
On/again
Off/again,
Lady,
And me multiplying the nights
That passed through your thighs:
The man-made things
The God-made things
Ground into gloom;
And shiny metal loves
Rusting in the cold relish of *I-told-you-so;*
Black love,
        vexatious passion,
Paused, perched in the violent crux —
Sung and stung, where the tremor
Is tailored to the pain
Of our white couch:
Does a whiteness separate us,
        /Blackwoman/?
Away from the headlines
And the cool cosmetics
        /Browngirl/
Golden in the sun's squint:
Woman-deep in worry
While infinite horrors stalk our need
While infinite tremors taunt our namesakes:
        tremors that bruised your thighs
        before I savored the rootjuices of your forests
        and the bark and limbbeginnings, greening greening;

This love/
        spastic heart in full gallop/
On/again/
Off/again:
Blistered seed groping toward a night called want
Hunched song in the throat of freedom;
And our love at stake? At the stake?
And the mind *one* body?
And the man *one* man? Against the cosmetics that coat us?
Against the wee-hour nightpeople
Who deep-freeze our urgency?
And this love/
On/again
Off/again . . .

HER BLACK BODY IN LIGHT

her blackbody in light of my need
her blackbody a wound in my eye
her blackbody the brail i rub
          /to know my blinding temperature/
blackbody in light
in special/spatial calibration
fleshglare/flashglow
her body inundate
nightdrum. silence. strumming.
skin
blackboy impaled
penis a scar

poised   /blackbody/   in light as hands in grace
in pricking light
in boomerang light
          /of teeth, of stars/
enameling light
quietlunging light
stealthing light

her *bodyglare*. black.
unanimity of her *severalness*
allah the sum of her parts

Blackwoman: facsimile of god
her body in glowlyre
in storm smiling
sun-fixed, sun-frequent
her blackbody in light
her twist a modification of horror
her sigh a knife in the open wound of want
her blackbody in light

STARFUCK

Screw out the stars;
Dimdown the moon —
Now:
      "What sign are you on, man?"
      "What sign are you under, woman?"

BRUSHFIRE

Yourbody   /voluptuous match/
Striking the flints-of-my-eyes:
Flame-pupils; jellfire — *Now!*
Love slumbers in sulphurous
Combustion/
Slumbers in fire-seeds
Slumbers in need waves.

... MORNING SO SOON, TOO SOON ...

I woke up this morning
        /my woman in my mouth/
Making lunch of left-over need
Oozing through a thigh —
My mind a barbed-wire camp of fear,
My privacy exposed to the silent gossip
Of nosey noiseless walls —
A dent beside me in the bed,
Ploughed sheets . . . one earring,
My chilled-filled arm amputated
Up to where your neck withdrew
From the refrigerator of night —
My eyes slits of soft fire
Sword-fighting the sun,
The moon mockingly hovering
In one window of a flashback:

Morning, Lord, so soon, too soon . . .

PASSION CHANT

Your tongue a torch in the night of my mouth:
Renders me an avenue for flame-travel:
O and my eyes are rainbows shuttered
In the wind of your breath —
    My love a tall lance, a knife of many edges!
    My love a hammer, forging souls in the dark!
    O trance O O need O trance O
Your webbed body Tarantula-Octopus-Eagle hum, O hum,
O hum, our love a lullaby beside the lake of,
        beside the godgrove!
    My love a tenderloin, my love a desperate river!
An engine in wind, O trance, a teeth-ground ecstasy,
        elasticity!
    O inclined body, upclimbed body!
    O marbles of sweat that bejeweled you!
Jewel-woman, your sigh a guitar chorus saucing my viscera:
And the faces of all my former orgasms gush from me —
From me, gush against the walls that dam your womb;
    And the moon, O moon, a silhouetted sperm,
    And I-the-sun in heat, heating the sun —
    And O my heart baked in the oven of your body:
    In the daughter-fires of this godwife, lady-furnace:
O you *the night*, O you *the night*, O you *the night!*
Walking gapped-legged through the pubic forest:
The pines! the oaks! of my erections!
And my love a collar in the crass cellar of stocks and bonds,
And my love a corridor between you; you a conduit & direct current;
A bush chant of openings; your mouth an effortless cave;
    My love an anchor, anger is my love, my love
    In anger saddled by your limb-cage-song —

Saddled by the syncopation of your thighs,
    By the moist re-orderings of my own sanity.
And my love — O eyes shut deathlike;
And my love staring through skin, through
Your succulent transparency;
And night,
        now,
A quiet howl sucked inside you —
Swept in with the debris of my body;
And you becoming, darling, the rhythm of my parts;
The night that would cement all the nights before —
And all winds, all rage gathered at your vortex;
And my love,
        sun-reproaching,
A Black jingle in the air!
A Black jingle in the air!

YOUR BREATH PHOTOGRAPHS THE WIND

Your breath photographs the wind&
Hums hums our picturesque emotions;
You breath photographs the wind&
Grooms a kaleidoscope of sighs:

Your breath a snare in a whirl
Your breath a clutch in my mouth
Your breath an oxygen-tent of tremors
Your breath a shiver in openings, in ears —

Your breath some polaroid of thought;
Some stretch of canvas-feel & want;
Some mural of whisper-goddesses & demons;
Some snapshot of palpitation & ventilation;
Some negative of naked ache & flame;
Some caricature of Godvoice & storm —

So, your breath photographs the wind&
Restores the chant to my tongue;
Your breath photographs the wind&
Nods in the hamlet of my throat!

Your breath photographs the wind&
Blows out the moon&
Fogs the windows of the sun&
Shutters the night of stars&
Shuts down the furnaces of my eyes —

And your breath photographs the wind!

LOVE AS ENIGMA: EYE

I know it's hard,
Blackwoman,
To thread the needle
Of my love:
To trace commitment
Beyond my capriciousness
　　Beyond all shadows
　　Beyond all doubts
— hard to angle your dossier of desire
Through the eyes of my storm
— to sew permanence
To sew impunity:
It's hard,
Blacklady,
To thread the needle
That sometimes numbs your ecstasy:
Yet bores and bores and bores;
Its point a *stealth!*
Its point a dormant *quake!*

Our needle of anxiety
　　Stitching and stalking
　　Stitching and stalking
A point on the pendulum
A sharp shadow on the face of dumbfounded need
An infinite incision in the heart
An invisible chill
A fear-fraught thrill:
And *quandary*, woman, and *quandary*
(the blindness of pain; the blitzing pain;
　the blindness of pace, of speed)
And your head a merry-go-round of gloom:
A whir, a blur on the outskirts of the storm/soul
In whose eye
The siamese twin of God,
In dilemma/in doubt,
Sees the changes
Sees and *seeds* the changes.

AGAIN, AGAIN

On the raceway
Of the struggle
I surge, again, out of myself
          /throttle open, hope open/
As starting blocks tremble,
Fall away,
And crumble in cinders of dry sweat
In the ashes
Of an energy
Of an energy resurrected by that *Old Time Religion;*
Deathless love
In the stretch,
Where artificial respiration will not work:
I call on the grandpassions
          /grandmyths/
To make me over and over
To catapult me to the next insurrection
          /the next erection!/
Of the soul!
Of the soul:
Where Nat Turner broods
In a basement bastille:
In the stretch,
I hurl back the yawns
          /the bores/
And the reptile-hiss of rhetoric
And the grief-shuttling gossip
And the knives drilled systematically into my back
By slower runners of the race
          /and by referees, by referees/;

Moving moving on the raceway of the struggle
Against the thoroughbreds of oppression
Against the quarterhorses of the king
Where lights grow dim in white houses
        /I insist/
When midnight cackles at the sun
        /I insist/
When gold boggles and dazzles
I rarify a love and,
Cuddling hope,
Carry a bolt of lightning in my hand.

LOVE AS NOSTALGIA;
LOVE AS REMEMBRANCE
Listening to *Horace Silver's* "Lonely Woman"

Trained hands at a keyboard
Carefully sprinkling shades of salt
Into the niches of an old love
Into the silk-masked wounds
Into the historical throbs —
The pain of piano nights
The pain of salty mornings
And a bass walks through the horror chambers
Of the museum of love;
The scales, the notes numb a visiting need:
Rekindle nostalgia and resurrect ghosts
Once ground into memory's junkyard —
Tried hands at the keyboard,
Plunking out acoustics of my pain:
Doubling as nostrils
That breed breath and asphixiate anxiety —
An old love
An old love
Wandering through smoke
Stumbling through smogged ideas
Wandering through the pollution of worry
Tiptoeing through quicksands of memory:
Tried hands narrow
To a crevice of desire
That nestles night
Down to burning blackflame
Whose final finger
Plucks the keyboard of conscience
Pricks the black & white notes of nostalgia —
Crowds a clandestine vacuum
In one wall of the heart
In one ventricle of memory
In one well of tears:
An old love
An old love

NIGHT GROWS

Night grows from
The seed-filled face
Of my woman
Whose neon eyes narrow
To Blacklites: ancestral beacons of search

Woman
On whose body little moons sprout
Woman
On whose body little galaxies grow

Night grows
From the face of my lady
As I grow in her valley
As I grope through her exquisite cities
As I scale the hillsides of her rural areas

Night grows
Night grows

COIL, BLACKWOMAN

Coil, coil
Blackwoman
Coil
Your cool stares
Around my misery

Stun me with
The jolt of your eyes
With the lightning rod of your looks
Coil your light
Into a lashless love
Into cinematic thunder
Into infra-red passion
Coil Blackwoman
Claim my territorial thoughts
Unfurl your flag on my phallus
Beam past my boundaries
Beam into these closed vaults
Beam into the crypts of my dormant malehood
Coil
Claw claw with your eyes
Your way through this brittle boyhood of armor
Into the man that only you know I am.

JAM BATTLE

With the oracular arrow
He wounded her
          /in nightflight/
Brought her
          /in heat, in crash/
To the flame-floor of his desire —
A fiery launching pad of creaking passion —
Which flared him
Into a bathroom troubador —
Strumming on morning —
Doing the Ali-shuffle in a cold shower:

While she slept
Between her own thighs
     His wallet in one hand
       His mind clasped in the slumbering other.

HIGHFLOWN: LOVE

In the highflown language
Of moon travelers
Social scientists sort our hurts —
Add their smog-crippled vision —
And rearrange our private pains
Along the Wall Street of current demands;
And my people become the
Cocaine that makes America high:
Become dreams
America sucks through maniacal straws of sleep;
Discounting our lore,
The scientists say we *cannot love*
                say our needs are numbed:
But sometimes,
When you construct knots in my throat
And your lips re-create my heartclock,
I am hypnotized by the aggregate passion
Of my past   by the sum of my historical ecstasy:
A power we know
Cannot be stilled by airborne theories of scholars
Nestled in Freudian citadels:
A power that cannot be seen
Heard
Or flattened to fit the pages of a book.

FUNKY–GRACE

MYTH VAULTER

From the Introduction to
Keith Jefferson's **Hyena Reader**,
March 22, 1976

Another Myth-vault, Keith/Jefferson —
Blackpiper, Wordquilter, Warmthbringer,
Wailteller, Deepreaper —
flaunts his
"Mr. 5 by 5"
"Clyde McPhatter"
"Bird"
with flinchless Soulo-Elegance:
> *Jazz takes it.*
> *Jazz takes it away.*
> *Jazz takes it apart. distinguishes*
> *the essentials*
> *from what would be mist.*
Rhymes anciently, this finesser,
for a questing/questing hyena
("who's laughing at who?");
talks of air that "wraps its shiny arms around me"
& how the "Pregnant aroma of living"
drives a dart-of-a-blackbody
whose "spine is a spear."

Jefferson knows the boards
and splinters of life:
"you like deep don't you night";
"veined ghetto"; "Untidy Cheetahs";
"through the nappy head of night" —
into eternal unw/rappings of love,
dispossession, lust and *Festivities*.

Jefferson, he lifts fog
from the brain and dust
from thirsty party floors:
Better yet, hear Keith Jefferson *Reed!*
Yaw Kay? . . . AlRite!

BYE-CENTENNIAL:
UNREFLECTED THRUSTS AND FRONTIERS
For *Ahaji Umbudi*

Drum & Fife
Drum & Fife
Zig America zag
Thru goulash and gumbo and oboe
Patchpatchwork HUM clock
Clockclocking: Tambourine underbump
HUM
HUM
Indelicacies into frontiers
New England
New Africa
New World wading in weeping in antique fears
HAIL!
HAIL!
The seismic lull of liberated *bells*

Post-toasties
Grape-nuts
Loan Rangers   Jumping frogs   Bluespeople
     Allegheny go-go   Stradivarian hoe-down   Expresso-bo-bo
Mumbling muskets   Ahab in search of Jonah   How kkkum?
     Black gold   Rock-a-my-soul in the bosom of slavery
Ramble of the Pre-amble   DRUM & FIFE   HUM HUM   Into frontiers
     Ace or Spade?   Harborer harborer pearls & harbors
Igloo   Angola & Reggae   Harvest moons/sniper moons
     Bus or Bust!

What did Hoo/doo
To get so black & blue

Zig zag
Zig zag

Celluloid transplants
Sutures on the liberty knell
Knockknockknock of night-leerers
                          come to order silence

HUM
HUM
Indelicacies into frontiers
Slapped leather & totemized saddles
Zigzagging hair-triggered lover
Heavyhymn of a naturalborn death-wish
Samboo-boo dance at JamesTown
Soot-stained Oedipal clutch of Jolson

The squeak/squeak of Watergate
Attucks-the-bullet-eater
Attucks-the-bullet-eater
Attucks-the-bullet-eater
Attucks-the-bullet-eater
Attucks-the-bullet-eater
Attucks-the-bullet-eater

HUM
HUM
Emphysema of the drum
Influenza of the fife

HUM HUM
HUM HUM

SURFACES

Yes,
Our umbilical bridge of love
Is mined with hurt-lumps,
Grenades of gossip,
Napalms of unconfirmed reports,
Guided missiles of racism.

But in the yesterzooms,
In the firefights of struggle,
We defeat the nerve-bombs bursting
In the chaotic belly of lassoed fury;
Defeat the visual screams,
Defeat the vocal photographs,
Defeat the sticky smell of acquiescence
              in our private temperature zones;
Knowing this
Knowing this
Knowing this
Standing for a store-window ethos is like being
              in a quizzical sophomore slumber;
Standing where no ground grows is haze-mire &
       clutter-sight,
              is perforated belief:
Unless we climb downward the natal-ladder of extra-
       anatomical
              concordance —
Unless we ride upward the elevator-root of soular
       instincts
              & inheritance — or soar
Rearward along the continuum of drumscript,

Our rapture will remain an inconsequential
        quiver, a dart
                of mimic-dust without mirrors
                            without seasons
                without space for silences, echoes,
                soulos & reflections.

PREMATURE CONVERSATION;
OR, WHAT WE SAID BEFORE WE TALKED

In din-din,
Thru tongue-clicks,
Over droning, self-actuated ecstasies/
    rumor-utter, rumor-utter, rumor-utter:
    In the cemetery of words & postulations/
I cautiously count imaginary monologues
(Framed by your fidgeting)
Assuming that
You too are dreaming open-eyed:
You too are wanting these garrulous invaders
Of our Sacred Galaxy to evaporate
Into the anonymity of night.

But you come no closer
As our excess audience declines retreat.
So the open-eyed dialog dumbs-dumbs
Us into indelible fractures,
Contorted tilt-glances that re-produce
Stare-dreams/silent ghost-screams
Of sweet-hesitant-terror.

Nevertheless, I need to stun you with
My torrents of intimacies and deliriums,
Grab-gore you with the soft-might
Of my teeth-gritting karma,
Kidnap you with lasers
Launched lavishly from my face,
To drown you in the quiet,
Holy infamy of snarling/
Visceral currents.

But I don't dare become the hunger in me:
Instead I wait for providence
To drumphone the frequency of my crisis;
Knowing that speaking thru
The hieroglyphics of gesture
Is like nibbling on the unknown —
In a place you've never been before —
At a time estranged
From the computation of clocks —
With a delicate fury more forthright
Than nerves —
On a transspatial plane that shuttles
The humming cargoes of my genital refrains
Into the waiting warehouse of silence.

FLIGHT FROM TEXARKANA TO DALLAS:
AIR EDIFICE
(Homage to an Ebony Filght Attendant)
August 20, 1977

In the aisle of a giant bee
      stinging and winging clouds
A dextrous, glory-angled, brown flame
Calmed and collected our
      unmumbled apprehensions
Into the cushioned hamlet of her face;

While the humid murmur-weep
Texas-gaped from the green yawn below:
      grace-girl: helm-lady,
      flesh-edifice . . .
Murmur-weep that clung
To sweating mirages aboard
This plantation in the air
      grace-girl
Where feebled or fancied hands
Clasped mint-juleps
Dispensed from the
Fingers of an ageless ark of flesh:
      grace-girl: helm-lady,
      ebony-edifice . . .
Double-fated flight: on which
Some sat snugly
Assured ancient order *prevailed* —
Even if tested by airborne
      freedom-marchers.

Less snug, and cautiously masking
Their bubbling elations,
The deeper-pitched passengers
Hailed *grace-girl* with
Silent praises and appellations:
Coolly rejoicing at this revolution —
Fleshingmagically before their eyes!
                    witnesses . . . witnesses

Meanwhile,
Jubilee-daughter —
Her soft armor impenetrable
As she led the silentchoral ascent —
Knew and unknew the
Cathartic turbulences
Illuminated by her aura:
Maintained her glory-limp —
            her lush electricity
            her charismatic cause
Remained & Remained:
Effortless in the Brilliant *Dream-amble:*
Inalienable, I tell you,
And Inevitable.

DOUBLE CLUTCH LOVER

". . . let me blues ya fo' I lose ya."
Southend saying, East St. Louis, Illinois

Her fury and her fire was in her cold-cold fame:
Double mojo-mama, Yeah, and Double Clutch Lover was her
    name.

She had the cold-cuttin fire, baby, she had the flame, the flame.

Her rep was hep — and she didn't mess with no lame —
        Her fire was in her fame!
        Her fire was in her fame!
O Yeah! Uh Huh! O Yeah! Uh Huh!
    Cause she was a double
I said a double // two barrels
I said a double // two barrels
    Make it two, babeeeee!
    Cause she was a Double Clutch Lover
And she could double clutch // clutch-clutch
        double clutch // clutch-clutch // your love
        Double-clutcher
        Double-clutcher

She was a, *ah, er-ruh*, triple dealer,
        And a — uuh-uhh — banana peeler,
                Yeah, a quick-shifting wheeler.
      Double-Clutch Pearl
      Kitchen-Grease Girl
Witch-woman-of-a-healer!

Fruit, funk and fire was in her cold, Lawd!, cold cuttin flame;
She kept comin, kept comin in Jesus' name!, Lawd!
    Double-Clutch Double-Clutch my love

She took my temperature with a two-foot tongue
That accelerated my engine when it reached my lung!
   Clutch-Clutch Double-Clutch
A break-fast filly that couldn't be tamed . . .
   Couldn't be tamed!
African back-bender that made the Holy Ghost shame:
  For Shame! Double-Clutch
  For Shame! Double-Clutch
Rump-queen that conquered the washing machine
   (Yeah, before it was invented!).
Washboard wonder-woman scrubbing her convictions,
Hand-clapping her way through old-time restrictions:
   Knuckle-Rubber
   Knuckle-Rubber
  Double-Clutch-Lover
  Double-Clutch-Lover . . .

Woman walked across fire and still didn't fidget!
   Walked across fire, *John Yo Henry,* and still didn't
   fidget!
  Dig it! Dig it!

Funk-junction lady with a jack-knife jump!
  I said a funk-junction lady with a jack-knife jump!
If you can't sprout your tree before she counts to three
  She might leave you with a stump:
Funk-junction lady with a jack-knife jump,
  Hump-hump // Hump-hump

Yeah!, yall, her fire, her fire, was in her cold-cold fame
Where Hard-Hearted Hanna couldn't stake no claim:

Double-Clutch-Lover
Double-Clutch-Lover
Lawd, make you run for cover . . .
  Hover-hover, baby, hover-hover.
She can gun you to the curb;
    Make you *scream-cry* for reverb!
Now ain't that some nerve!
    Girl got nerve!
Double-clutch woman armed with life —
Double-Clutcher, yeah, armed to the teeth with life, Lawd!
    Expert on Strife!
    Expert on Strife!
A triple dealer!
Banana peeler!
Quick-shifting wheeler!
    Double-Clutch-Lover
  Run for cover, man,
  Run for cover, man:
Keeps her foot on my pedal —
    Pushin-clutchin // pushin-clutchin
Keeps her hand on the throttle of life,
    Expert on Strife, Throttle of Life, Expert on Strife.
    Pushin-clutchin // Pushin-clutchin
    Pushin-clutchin // Pushin-clutchin

FUNKY-GRACE

(From *The Hero Series*)
For *Joseph E. Harrison*

He took the lion-lunge,
Hey! Hey!
He took the tiger-step,
Hey! Hey!
He took the tomb-trail,
Hey! Hey!
He took the sacred-plunge.
Hey! Hey!

He made the ocean-leap!
Hey! Hey!
He made the gong/gong-call!
Hey! Hey!
He made the death-mouth,
Hey! Hey!
He made the freedom-creep.
Hey! Hey!

He ate the juicy-blues!
Hey! Hey!
He ate the rat/roach flat!
Hey! Hey!
He ate the numb-stare,
Hey! Hey!
He ate the airborn-shoes!
Hey! Hey!

He caught the sassy-space!
Hey! Hey!
He caught the totem-call!
Hey! Hey!
He caught the kill-flame!
Hey! Hey!
He caught the Funky-Grace!
Hey! Hey!
He caught that Funky-Grace!
Hey! Hey!
He caught that Funky-Grace!
Hey! Hey!

SEARCHING THE BODY FOR WOUNDS

Somersaulting backwards from life's noisy rim,
I consult with utter breath — that song brocaded
In the whirl-lore of self-address:
           Crouching-whispering lovers —
           Crouching, cringe-whispering lovers;
Lunging lunging into the fidgeting interior
Of lonesome & leering circumstance —
Where war-splattered convenors exile themselves:
           Wailing lovers in the limbs of fire!
           Wailing lovers in the limbs of fire!
And left-handed justices dispense grief
From candy-counters of Reward & Punishment;
Where tears are dusty dreams . . .
Where tears are dusty dreams . . .
           Crouch-wailers in their fire-quick need!
           Crouch-wailers in their fire-quick need!
Where hard-bargaining angels of pain
Smash opium-masks of high-styled ecstasy
And the scars of our aging odyssey reclaim their salty truths:
           No hiding place but a mourning tree!
           No hiding place but a mourning tree!
Where I frisk myself,
Indulge in dark massages,
Inch-inch over my own body in search of other wounds:
           Stalking the historical tightrope!
Engage in gross combat: self-pummeling-self,
In a prize-fight with the invincible gladiator inside me.

NEW YORK SEIZURES

For *Raymond Patterson*

#1

I sit in a glass submarine
Watching contortion consume beauty:
  as flesh inches toward dust and oblivion,
  ... a-what-a-ya-wanna, eh!? a-what-a-ya-wanna!
  As flesh inches toward the next corner of tumult —
To where wrinkled octogenarians,
  Spontaneous in their gloom,
Stagger-stab the grimacing city blocks
With lock-legged steps;
And broken winds exhale columns of creaking
Epilogues from eyes without age ...

   No dozer, no-doze city and never-wink wailer,
   Babbling through your Benzedrine and beer!

#2

Now disguised as a street lamp,
I am whiplashed/whiplashed into serpentine ecstasy
By lush scenarios
By concrete choruses
  And asphalt furies:
By the snaking quarrel of bi-lingual taxi-cabs —

   Where the night turns yellow!
   Where New York gets mel-looow!

—And perspiring tenements:

Toombs for pre-people returning home
From mystical voyages to be somebody;

By the hover-clusters of chuckling midgets
Who hurl diabolical ringshouts under thunder-tears
Of Gleeful gods: Apollo, Shango, John Henry & Bobo —
And rocket naughty clichés at bronze brickhouses,
Headhunters
Plush stallions,
Stark-denyers of identities,
Penis-flingers
Cunt-lubricators,
Sweetboys
& Blood-borrowers:

> *eenie meenie mynie mo las night/night befo*
> *spin yo bottom shoot yo shot keep her'n creep her*
> *let me blues ya fo I lose ya let me try ya*
> *'fo I buy ya I got the jones 'nnn if you got*
> *the bones dick haarrddd as Chinese Arithmetic*
> *ya know I ain't tawkin bout yo momma wit hu good*
> *o soul . . . uh uhhh! uh uhhhh! uh uhhhhhhh!*

#3

The neighborhood nextdoor is hallucinating:
Woman says she saw a BlackJesus riding in a WhiteHog
Wearing a Green jumpsuit and holding two BrownFoxes;
A platinum barrel of death stares into the stomach
Of a short-order cook demanding the cashregister & life — *to go!*
A gentleman who wears low profiles tells his woman
That she makes love like his best buddy;

A Puerto Rican speaks Voodoo with an African accent;
A European speaks African with a Spanish accent;
A West Indian yawns in Yiddish and curses in Arabic;
An African speaks English in silence;
A slave revolt occurs under the cover of a blackout;
Color-crossed lovers hold hands in cross-eyed Central Park;
Subway trains are flying nonStop to South Africa;
Harlem has received the Nobel Prize for Peace;
Mountain climbers are trying to scale the City Debt;
The Indians are hijacking the Empire State Building;
This winter's snow turns out to co-caine.

#4

Lucid lumbrous eye
            New York;
Luminous fragments,
            Like New Year's Eve tin-foils,
            Collect into an epidemic of flesh-ignited candles
That refuse to go out —
Even when the temperamental gods of Con-Edison are comatose;

Whir-City,heat forest
Of memorable fevers,
            Asphalt icon:

Jezzibel mesmerizer,
Sleep-exempt entrancer:
I rap-prance my congratulations on the achievement of your
excellent
            madness,
On the triumph of your pretty contradictions;

I tap-dance my salutes through your basement of shuttles and barbiturates;
I clop-clop along your rib-cage of cobblestones;
I pee-pee in the wee-wee hours of your doorways;
I mee-lee in your disco-drudgery;
I be-me in your awesome amber:

> No dozer, no-doze city & never-wink wailer,
> Babbling through your Benzedrine and beer!

EUGENE B. REDMOND holds both a B.A. and M.A. degree in English Literature. He is a prize-winning poet-teacher-journalist who has combined a teaching and writing career with active participation in Black community development. His writings have appeared in publications in Africa, Europe, and the United States. He was a contributing editor to the weekly East St. Louis Monitor newspaper, and to Confrontation: A Journal of Third World Literature.

He has published the following books of poems:

SENTRYOFTHEFOURGOLDENPILLARS	(1970)
RIVERS OF BONES AND FLESH AND BLOOD	(1971)
SONGS FROM AN AFRO/PHONE	(1972)
IN A TIME OF RAIN & DESIRE: NEW LOVE POEMS	(1973)
CONSIDER LONELINESS AS THESE THINGS	(1974)